The Confederacy's First Battle Flag

The Confederacy's First Battle Flag

First Battle Flag

THE STORY OF THE SOUTHERN CROSS

Kent Masterson Brown

With the assistance of Lon W. Keim, MD

PELICAN PUBLISHING COMPANY
Gretna 2014

Library of Congress Cataloging-in-Publication Data

Brown, Kent Masterson, 1949-
  The Confederacy's first battle flag : the story of the southern cross / by
Kent Masterson Brown, with the assistance of Lon W. Keim, MD.
    pages cm
  ISBN 978-1-4556-1894-1 (pbk. : alk. paper) — ISBN 978-1-4556-1895-
8 (e-book) 1. Flags—Confederate States of America. 2. United States—
History—Civil War, 1861-1865--Flags. I. Keim, Lon W. II. Title.
  CR113.5.B76 2014
  929.9'20973—dc23

                        2013046434

Printed in the United States of America

Published by Pelican Publishing Company, Inc.
1000 Burmaster Street, Gretna, Louisiana 70053

Affectionately, to four great ladies of the South,

Mary Henry Lyon Jones,
Hetty Carr Cary,
Jane Margaret "Jennie" Cary,
Constance Fairfax Cary,

and to

Howard Michael Madaus,

who first introduced all of us
to Mary Henry Lyon Jones

Contents

Introduction

The story of the first Confederate St. Andrew's Cross battle flag, the prototype of all other such flags, became known in the 1980s when Lon W. Keim, MD, of Omaha, Nebraska, acquired what was believed to be that flag for his birthday! It was a square banner, made of two pieces of red silk with a deep-blue silk St. Andrew's Cross edged in white. The stars were painted on the cross in gold. Embroidered on the flag were the words "Shiloh" in the upper quadrant and "Perryville" in the lower. It seemed odd then that a Confederate St. Andrew's Cross battle flag that was the prototype for all other such flags would have been carried in the Western campaigns. But all of what was said about that flag proved to be true. No less a historian than the late Howard "Howie" Michael Madaus dredged out of the Louisiana Historical Association Papers at Tulane University in New Orleans the basic story of that flag. Howie tragically passed away in 2007 at only sixty-four years of age; he left behind, though, the fragments of a story as absorbing and colorful as any in the rich annals of the American Civil War. It is hard to imagine that this is the first book ever written on this subject.

Witnessing History, LLC, a film-production company in Lexington, Kentucky, produced a documentary in 2013 on the famed battle flag that Howie had identified, calling the film *The Southern Cross: The Story of the Confederacy's First Battle Flag*. It can be seen on public and cable channels, as well as wireless services everywhere. This is the companion book; it expands considerably upon Howie's initial efforts, filling in facts that he was unable to recover during his tragically shortened life. It is upon the back of a true giant in Civil War vexillological inquiry, Howie Madaus, that this book has been written. It is the fervent hope and prayer of the author that it will delight readers as much as it has delighted him.

Beyond Howie, there have been many people and institutions that have made this book possible. Nothing could have been accomplished without the use of the Louisiana Historical Association Papers at the Howard-Tilton Memorial Library at Tulane University. In those collections are all the letters collected by the Washington Artillery of New Orleans camp of the United Confederate Veterans and their Memorial Hall of the Crescent City. Some of those letters were written by the very men who first determined the army should have a St. Andrew's Cross banner and who acted upon that determination, including using Mary Henry Lyon Jones to stitch together the first such flag. From there, the Virginia State Library in Richmond provided material on the life of Mary Henry Lyon Jones and her husband, James Alfred Jones. Also in Richmond are the Museum of the Confederacy and its curator, John Coski, an old friend. That museum's collection of Confederate battle flags, ably overseen by my friend Drury Wellford, is beyond anything anyone can imagine, and its archives are incomparable. The Museum of the Confederacy has provided terrific images of battle flags, personalities, and documents, including images of the battle flags made by Hetty and Constance Cary. I could not write anything on the Confederate army in Virginia without asking my longtime friend Lewis Leigh, Jr., of Leesburg, Virginia, if his extensive collection of ephemera contained anything of interest. Here, naturally, it did. He possesses the original letters between Jennie Cary and Gen. P.G.T. Beauregard regarding the battle flag Jennie made for the general. His collection also contains the original signed General Order Number 75 of November 28, 1861, issued when the first battle flags were presented to the regiments of the Confederate Army of the Potomac! Also, my dear friend the late William A. Turner, whose extensive Civil War collection included the largest assemblage of photographs of members of the Fifth Company of the Washington Artillery of New Orleans, freely allowed their use here only weeks before he passed away. Thanks cannot be said enough to all of them.

For providing wonderful imagery of people, places, and items pertinent to this story, I want to thank the Alabama Department of Archives and History, Montgomery; the Louisiana State Museum, Baton Rouge (which provided the image of the battle flag made by Jennie Cary); Louisiana State University Special Collections, Baton Rouge; the Virginia Historical Society; Richmond; the Library of Congress; the National Archives; as well as the Smithsonian Institution, Washington, DC. Don Troiani of Historical Art Prints has provided an example of his unparalleled artwork in his painting that embellishes this book. And Blain Piper of Fredericksburg, Virginia, and his partner, Judie Flowers of Portsmouth, Virginia, have provided the incredible photographic images of Hetty and Jennie Cary; neither has ever been published before.

There are many more who helped in this endeavor. The Shiloh National Military Park, Savannah, Tennessee; and the Perryville Battlefield State Historic Site, Perryville, Kentucky, and its superintendent, Kurt Holman, provided information and photographs.

Special thanks are due to the direct and collateral descendants of Mary Henry Lyon Jones: Mary Morris Gamble Booth of Lynchburg, Virginia; Mary Lyon Booth Verlin of Jacksonville, Florida; William M. Lyon, Jr., of Mobile, Alabama; and James Alfred Jones Tyler, Jr., of Charles City County, Virginia. They have provided the lovely portraits of Mary Henry Lyon Jones and James Alfred Jones as well as copies of the letters of both of them. They have also provided timely and important information about the Lyon and Jones families. If Mary was as lovely, kind, and generous as all of her descendants—and I know she was—she was a truly remarkable lady.

My old friend Lon W. Keim, MD, made this book possible by commissioning it. He is the executive producer of the documentary film as well. We have been friends for more than thirty years; I recall the day "Mickey," as we call him, acquired the flag. He was a close friend to Howie. I remember, with great fondness, my long association with both.

But Mickey was more than the one who acquired the flag. For years after he got it, he combed libraries for information about the flag and Mary Henry Lyon Jones. It was he who mined the

Louisiana Historical Association Papers and the collections of the Virginia State Library and then got to know the direct and collateral descendants of Mary Henry Lyon Jones and James Alfred Jones. They opened to him another world of letters and portraits. Mickey had taken what Howie had uncovered and turned it into a vast collection of material. That made this book possible.

My secretary, Sharon Howard, deserves a medal; she typed all the drafts and re-drafts and put up with my fidgeting over all of it. Likewise, my wife, Genevieve, and my children, Annie Louise, Philip, and Thomas, had to deal with my absence—physical and otherwise—in the writing of this story. Thank you all very much for your patience and understanding.

Finally, thanks are truly due to Nina Kooij, Erin Classen and Pelican Publishing Company for their interest in publishing this story and their supreme patience. That, of course, finally made this book possible.

The Confederacy's First Battle Flag

Chapter One

"[They] Had Set Their Hearts Upon the Southern Cross"

In the long experience of mankind, it may be safely said that whenever man espoused a cause, he created a flag—a banner— to celebrate it or to use defending it. When eleven slave states seceded from the Union and formed a new confederacy in late 1860 and in 1861, one of the great discussions among people of each seceded state, and of the Confederacy as a whole, was what flag they would fly.

During the months leading up to the secession of South Carolina from the Union, a profusion of flags appeared throughout that state. Most called to mind the state's Revolutionary War experience, incorporating the palmetto tree and crescent moon on a blue or white field. When the South Carolina Secession Convention met in the First Baptist Church in Columbia to consider an ordinance of secession on December 17, 1860, a flag was observed by a reporter from the *Charleston Daily Courier*:

> A beautiful silk flag, of blue ground with gilt fringe presented by a lady of Charleston, was suspended over the State House, bearing on one side the words "South Carolina Convention 1860." On the reverse a Palmetto, and at the trunk an open Bible, with the following: "God is our refuge and our strength, a very present help in time of trouble; therefore will we not fear; though the earth be removed, and though the mountains be carried into the sea. The Lord of Hosts is with us, the God of Jacob is our refuge."[1]

Smallpox broke out in Columbia, causing the secession convention to move to Charleston. There, in Institute Hall, and

15

The Charleston Secession Convention, December 20, 1860, a woodcut.
(Courtesy of the Library of Congress)

then in the smaller St. Andrew's Hall on Meeting Street, the
delegates reconvened. Patriotic emblems hung from poles and
lines all over the city. A liberty pole stood at the corner of Hayne
and Meeting Streets. The Pavilion Hotel at the corner of Meeting
and Hasell Streets displayed a banner depicting Hiram Powers'
statue of John C. Calhoun holding a shattered tablet with the
inscribed words: "Truth, Justice, and the Constitution." Calhoun
appeared on the banner to be looking down from the clouds;
below his figure were the words: "Behold its Fate."[2]

Another banner was spotted by a Charleston newspaper
reporter who noted: "Over the president's chair was suspended a
scarlet banner, with a blue quarter, emblazoned with the ancient
crescent and the Lone Star." A third banner hung on a line from
the officer's quarters of the Lower Guard House at the corner of
Meeting and Broad Streets across the intersection to city hall.

It also featured an illustration of Powers' statue of Calhoun, but portrayed South Carolina as the cornerstone of an edifice of Southern states, with the words: "BUILT FROM THE RUINS." Later, on December 20, that banner was taken down and hung above the dais in Institute Hall.[3]

Beneath that flag, the delegates voted to rescind South Carolina's ratification of the Constitution and dissolve the state's union with the United States on December 20, 1860. The voting took only eight minutes. David F. Jamison, president of the secession convention, tallied the votes and then, at 1:15 p.m., said in a loud voice: "I proclaim the State of South Carolina an Independent Commonwealth." Wild cheering echoed through the hall and could be heard up and down Meeting Street.[4]

In the larger Institute Hall the delegates signed the Ordinance of Secession. Institute Hall, the grand edifice of the South Carolina Institute, was built in the mid-1850s for operas and concerts, as well as the annual fairs of the institute itself. Elaborately decorated with emblems of the palmetto tree, classical figures, rice, cotton, and symbols of commerce by none other than artist Vivio Garibaldi, the nephew of Italian hero Giuseppe Garibaldi, Institute Hall was a magnificent backdrop to South Carolina's most historic moment. The document having been signed in front of the huge assemblage, William Edward Martin, clerk of the South Carolina Senate for over twenty years, walked onto Meeting Street and read aloud South Carolina's Ordinance of Secession. He concluded by calling for three cheers "for the separate Commonwealth of South Carolina." The new "commonwealth" needed a flag.[5]

One flag that was advocated by many as a banner for the new commonwealth was reported by the press as appearing in Charleston after the secession convention. The flag appears to have been the South Carolina "Lone Star" flag. It consisted of a red field bearing a single, white, five-pointed star. There were others. As early as December 3, 1860, *Charleston Mercury* published a number of suggestions for a potential flag. "Let her standard be," it wrote, "the simple scarlet, with fifteen stars. True, it will be a star spangled banner—but with nothing of the barber pole about it."[6]

Even earlier, on November 10, 1860, the *Mercury* suggested "a plain scarlet field, powdered with fifteen stars, white or yellow, according to fancy." Thought to be presented by the same "enthusiastic friend of the *Mercury*," another flag had been suggested on November 13: "A scarlet field, powdered with fifteen white stars, without stripes or eagles, intended to typify the future Confederacy of fifteen sovereign southern slave states." South Carolinians firmly believed that every one of the fifteen slave states in the Union would secede and join Carolina.[7]

One of the very popular flags was sewed together by a group of ladies in Charleston just before the vote on the Ordinance of Secession. The flag—actually a large swallowtail pennant—was eight feet long and six feet wide. The field was "turkey [blood] red," with "an immense white star in the center and a white crescent in the left-hand corner." On the morning after the secession vote, the giant flag was hoisted over the Customs House at the end of Broad Street on East Bay Street.[8]

Out of all the variations for a flag proposed before and after the secession convention, the Latin cross emblem emerged as the one of choice, particularly in South Carolina. The "Washington Artillery" of the Charleston militia (not to be confused with the famed Washington Artillery of New Orleans or with Capt. James F. Hart's South Carolina Battery, which was also known as the Washington Artillery) assembled on the parade ground of the Citadel in Charleston after the secession convention carrying a flag that was described by the *Charleston Mercury*:

> The flag is a red field, expressive of defiance, traversed by the blue cross of Carolina, with the lone star at the intersection. The inner and upper quarter of the field bears the word "READY" surmounted by the palmetto.[9]

The Washington Artillery was not alone. The Charleston Zouave Cadets had a similar flag. Reported the *Charleston Daily Courier* on December 22, 1860:

> When the first gun, "Old Secession," announced the secession of the State, they flung to the breeze the beautiful flag which now floats over their gymnasium. It is a red field, quartered with a blue cross, on which is a lone star (others will be added as [states] come into the Southern Constellation). On the upper quarter is the Palmetto, on the lower a savage looking tiger head.

The Washington Artillery and the Charleston Zouave Cadets were soon sent to occupy Castle Pinckney, an impressive, stone bastion fort that defended the channel of Charleston Harbor closest to the city.[10]

On Christmas Day 1860 the "Charleston Correspondent" for the *New York Herald* reported the earliest account of what came to be known as the "sovereignty flag." Designed by an unknown Charleston woman, it was a rectangular flag with a cruciform—or "Latin cross"—design consisting of blue horizontal arms and vertical arms with four five-pointed stars across both horizontal arms and three across both vertical arms, with one large five-pointed star in the center of the cross. In the upper-left quadrant of the flag were the palmetto and crescent emblems of South Carolina. A woodcut of the flag appeared in the *Herald*. That was followed by another depiction of the flag in the *Illustrated London*

The sovereignty flag, a woodcut. (Courtesy of the Library of Congress)

News on February 2, 1861. Wrote the *Illustrated London News*, "This is, we believe, the first flag which has been put forward by either of the seceding States." The sovereignty flag was very popular in South Carolina. So popular was it that it became known there, and in other areas of the southland, as "the Southern Cross." Although not formally adopted by South Carolina as its flag after secession, it may be considered as having been informally adopted by the people of the state.[11]

Interestingly, a sovereignty flag was actually raised over Alumni Hall of Yale University in New Haven, Connecticut, by a student from the South who was enrolled in the college. Another student, Charles Lee Foster, reported the incident to *Frank Leslie's Illustrated Newspaper*, which published an illustration of the flag flying over Alumni Hall on the same day that the *Illustrated London News* published its illustration.[12]

No flag was officially adopted by the seceded state of South Carolina, though, until January 26, 1861. The flag that was actually adopted was hardly like the sovereignty flag. Rather, it was a blue flag with a large white oval in the center. In the white oval was the palmetto tree, and in the upper-left corner of the flag was a white crescent. The flag's authorization lasted two days! On January 28, the State Legislature changed the flag again. This time, the flag it adopted was blue with a white palmetto tree in the center and a white crescent in the upper-left corner, altogether not too dissimilar to the flag of the State of South Carolina today.[13]

The months of January and February 1861 have been referred to as the great "Secession Winter," as, one-by-one, the Gulf states seceded from the Union. Mississippi seceded from the Union on January 9, Florida on January 10, Alabama on January 11, Georgia on January 19, Louisiana on January 26, and Texas on February 1. Within a space of forty-two days, seven states, from South Carolina to Texas, had seceded from the Union.[14]

During the height of the secession of the Gulf states, a profusion of secession flags appeared. The flag that hung at the secession convention in Alabama had a blue field lined with gold fringe; in the center of the flag was the figure of "Liberty," dressed in red, holding a flag in her left hand and a sword in her right. Over Liberty were the words: "INDEPENDENT NOW AND FOREVER."[15]

A secession rally in Savannah Georgia, a woodcut. (Courtesy of the Library of Congress)

Many of those early flags bore a strong resemblance to the Stars and Stripes. When Louisiana seceded from the Union on January 26, 1861, a flag appeared bearing six five-pointed, white stars in a blue field representing the seceded states of South Carolina, Florida, Georgia, Alabama, Mississippi, and Louisiana; thirteen alternating red and white stripes completed the flag. That secession flag was a copy of the Stars and Stripes; it illustrated the attachment many Southerners had to the old Union. The seceded states of Florida and Louisiana would adopt flags that were similar to the Stars and Stripes. In spite of their urge to leave the Union, many Southerners embraced the history they had in common with the United States and consciously sought to model their emblems to resemble those of the old Union.[16]

On February 1, 1861 the delegates from the six Southern states that had proclaimed their independence from the United States met in the capitol building in Montgomery, Alabama to form a new confederacy. The popular sentiment there—but not necessarily elsewhere in the Confederacy—was that the main features of the old United States Constitution should be incorporated into the Confederate Constitution and that, to give expression to that fact, the flag of the Confederacy should closely resemble that of the Stars and Stripes.[17]

The capitol building where the delegates hammered out a constitution and set about forming a new government was an imposing building. Built on a hill overlooking the city of Montgomery, Alabama, the capitol building faced the main thoroughfare of the city, Market Street. The three-story, neoclassical structure was made of plastered brick, scored to resemble stone. Its dome was rust colored and across the front was a three-story-high portico supported by six Corinthianesque columns. Atop the portico was an immense clock. The unkempt capitol grounds were defined by an iron fence that was missing sections. The capitol building faced Market Street; one half mile away was Court Square, the business district, where there was a large artesian well enclosed by an iron fence.[18]

It was on the second-floor veranda of the capitol building, framed by the giant columns, that Jefferson Davis was sworn in as president of the Confederacy on February 18, 1861. Illustrating the fact that the Confederacy had no unique, identifying flag, over the capitol building flew the flag of the State of Alabama, and Davis's inaugural procession was led by a company of infantry carrying the flag of the State of Georgia. The old capitol building in Montgomery would serve as the Confederate Capitol until the seat of government was moved to Richmond, Virginia, at the end of May 1861, a move that began, in essence, with a resolution offered by Francis S. Bartow of Georgia on May 11.[19]

On February 9, 1861, Christopher Memminger, a delegate from South Carolina, brought to the attention of the Provisional Congress in the capitol at Montgomery two different flag designs, one of which he called a "sovereignty flag." Made by the young ladies of Charleston, this flag was "much admired." That proposal resembled the Latin cross design so popular in South Carolina. It had a red field with a blue cross "studded with seven white stars," just like the original sovereignty flag. Another was a design that consisted of a blue cross with fifteen stars on a field of red and white stripes. Submitting the proposals, Memminger stated:

The inauguration of Jefferson Davis as president of the Confederacy, February 18, 1861, at the State Capitol, Montgomery, Alabama. (Courtesy of the Alabama Department of Archives and History, Montgomery, Alabama)

Mr. President, the idea of a union, no doubt was suggested to the imagination of the young ladies by the beauteous constellation of the Southern Cross, which the great Creator has placed in the southern heavens, by way of compensation for the glorious constellation at the north pole. The imagination of the young ladies was, no doubt, inspired by the genius of Dante and the scientific skill of Humbolt. But, sir, I have no doubt that there was another idea associated with it in the minds of the young ladies—a religious one—and although we have not seen in the heavens the "in hoc signo vinces," written upon laburnum of Constantine, yet the same sign has been manifested to us upon the tablets of the earth; for we all know that it has been by the aid of revealed religion that we have achieved over the fanaticism the victory which we this day witness; and it is beckoning, on this occasion, that the debt of the South to the cross should be thus recognized.

I have also, Mr. President, a commission from a gentleman of taste and skill in the city of Charleston, who offers another model, which embraces the same idea of a cross, but upon a different ground. The gentleman who offers this model appears more hopeful than the young ladies. They offer one with seven stars—six of the States already represented in the Congress, and the seventh for Texas, whose deputies we hope will soon be on their way to join us. He offers a flag which embraces the whole fifteen States. God grant that this hope may soon be realized, and that we may soon welcome their stars to the glorious constellation of the Southern Confederacy.[20]

Another proposal submitted to the Provisional Congress included a blue Latin cross containing white stars with a red field not too dissimilar from the sovereignty flag. Wrote the *Charleston Daily Courier* on February 15, 1861:

The "Southern Cross" is a favorite with many citizens whose opinions have reached us, and has been presented in a variety of forms, by a gentleman of this city, who proposed it, we believe, soon after, if not before, the secession of South Carolina.[21]

The flag that emerged in Congress was designed by Nichola Marschall of Marion, Alabama. Marschall was born in St. Wendel, Germany, in 1829. His family were well-to-do tobacco merchants. He immigrated to the United States in 1849 through New Orleans and took up residence in the home of a relative in Mobile, Alabama. In 1851 Marschall relocated to Marion, where he began teaching art at his own studio and at the Marion Female Seminary. He also painted portraits commercially. Marschall briefly returned to Germany to continue his own training but journeyed back to Marion before the outbreak of the Civil War.[22]

Marschall's flag consisted of two horizontal red stripes and a center white stripe with a blue field containing a circle of white, five-pointed stars representing the Confederate states. It became known far and wide as the "Stars and Bars," for it bore a strong resemblance to the Stars and Stripes. On March 4, 1861, the Stars and Bars flag was adopted by the Provisional Confederate Congress. It was raised over the capitol building by Miss Letitia Christian Tyler, the granddaughter of Pres. John Tyler, that same day.[23]

The Stars and Bars was met with mixed reviews in the Confederacy. The *Charleston Mercury* reported the first appearance of the new flag:

The National Ensign of the Confederate States of America was displayed yesterday from the flagstaff over the cupola of the Customs House [in Charleston]. It attracted a great deal of attention, and various opinions were expressed concerning it. Some thought it too much like the United States flag—others had set their hearts upon the 'Southern Cross' being somehow embodied in our new banner.[24]

When Maj. Robert H. Anderson surrendered his Federal garrison at Fort Sumter to Gen. Pierre Gustave Toutant Beauregard on April 13, 1861, the Confederate forces took over the fort at the mouth of Charleston Harbor. Before anything further was done in the captured fort, the jubilant Confederates raised an immense Stars and Bars flag along with the palmetto flag of South Carolina. The Stars and Bars and the South Carolina palmetto flag fluttered over the bastion of the new Confederacy.[25]

One member of the Provisional Confederate Congress who objected to the Stars and Bars was William Porcher Miles of South Carolina, the chairman of the House Military Committee. Miles, born on July 4, 1832, was the son of a plantation family from Walterboro in the Colleton District of South Carolina. He

Fort Sumter after the surrender of the Federal garrison on April 13, 1861, showing the Stars and Bars flying over the damaged fort. (Courtesy of the Library of Congress)

was graduated from the College of Charleston in 1842. Although admitted to the bar, Miles chose a career teaching mathematics at his alma mater, where he served as an assistant professor from 1843 until 1855. He became mayor of Charleston in 1855 and then was elected to Congress in 1857. Miles served in Congress until South Carolina seceded from the Union in December 1860; he then served as a delegate to the South Carolina Secession Convention and was elected to the Provisional Confederate Congress as well as the First and Second Congresses of the permanent Confederate government. In 1863, Miles would marry the former Elizabeth Bevine, the daughter of a Virginia planter with large land holdings in the Old Dominion as well as Louisiana.[26]

Miles regarded the United States flag as the emblem of a tyrannical government. He preferred a red flag bearing a blue heraldic emblem—the saltire, or St. Andrew's Cross—with inner rows of stars. "The saltire," reported the *Charleston Mercury*, echoing Miles' contentions, "is the symbol of strength," and the stars, which in Miles' original drawings were six-pointed stars known as étoiles, represented the Confederate states. The House Military Committee, however, flatly rejected Miles' effort to change the Confederate flag.[27]

The saltire was, in fact, the oldest emblem of sovereignty in the Western world, having its origins with the Scotts maybe as early as AD 832. It was used by the Romans in Britain as a boundary emblem years before then. The word *saltire* is derived from the Latin "salto," meaning "to leap" or "to jump," and it was applied to the boundary emblems as the Roman Empire's expansion into Britain and elsewhere was recorded by the placement of those emblems along the empire's ever-widening frontier.[28]

The saltire of Miles' design was also known as the St. Andrew's Cross, named in honor of the first-century Christian martyr who was crucified on a saltire. It was said St. Andrew's remains were sent to the Scottish coast in the fourth century. St. Andrew became the patron saint of Scotland; his cross became the nation's symbol. The St. Andrew's Cross was incorporated into the British Union Jack when King James VI of Scotland became King James I of England.[29]

Col. James Burdge Walton, commander of the Washington Artillery Battalion of New Orleans, a carte-de-visite photograph. (Courtesy of the Alabama Department of Archives and History, Montgomery, Alabama)

In April 1861 Col. James Burdge Walton, commander of the famed battalion of the Washington Artillery of New Orleans, requested newspaperman Edward C. Hancock of New Orleans to draw a proposed group of flags for Confederate military purposes. Hancock's proposal consisted of a color rendition of a flag with a rectangular field of red. It apparently resembled the sovereignty flag, having a red field and a dark blue Latin cross with white stars quartering the field horizontally and vertically.[30]

Although Hancock completed his drawings, they were never sent to the House Military Committee of the Provisional Congress in Montgomery, Alabama. Knowing there was to be a transfer of the seat of government from Montgomery to Richmond, Virginia, Maj. Walton carried Hancock's drawings with him when the original four companies of the Washington Artillery Battalion were transferred to Richmond in May 1861. Walton recalled: "I carried . . . the design to [Richmond], where it was freely exhibited and generally approved. Among others, it was shown to Colonel [William] Porcher Miles, a member of our flag committee."[31]

What finally underscored the need for a change, though, was the use of the Stars and Bars—and the widespread use of a multitude state flags—by Confederate regiments on the battlefield.

Chapter Two

"It Was Soon, However, Discovered to Be a Regiment of the Enemy"

When the Confederate and Federal armies collided outside of Manassas Junction, Virginia, on July 21, 1861, the need for a distinctive and uniform battle flag became urgent. The First Battle of Manassas involved the Confederate Armies of the Potomac and the Shenandoah, commanded by Gens. Pierre Gustave Toutant Beauregard and Joseph E. Johnston, respectively, together over 36,000 strong.[1]

General Beauregard, a native of St. Bernard Parish, Louisiana, was an 1838 graduate of West Point. After service with Gen. Winfield Scott during the Mexican War, he was assigned to be superintendent of the United States Military Academy in January 1861. Relieved shortly thereafter, Beauregard resigned his commission in the United States Army and was named a brigadier general in the Provisional Army of the Confederate States on March 1, 1861. He was placed in command at Charleston, South Carolina, and supervised the bombardment of Fort Sumter, the Federal garrison of which surrendered to him on April 13, 1861. As the widely-acclaimed hero of Fort Sumter, Beauregard was placed in command of Confederate forces in northern Virginia two months later.[2]

Beauregard named his force the Army of the Potomac. With the steady buildup of Federal forces in Washington, DC, and across the Potomac River in Arlington, Virginia, and the slow but steady advance of their outposts westward, Beauregard's army had retired from Fairfax County by July 17. The troops instead took a line along generally wooded heights overlooking a stream known as Bull Run, about three miles north of Manassas Junction.[3]

Because of the looming threat posed by the Federal forces outside of the city of Washington, the Confederate War Department looked to Gen. Joseph E. Johnston's Army of the Shenandoah to reinforce Beauregard's army. Johnston was born near Farmville, Virginia; he was a classmate of Robert E. Lee's at West Point, graduating in 1829. After service in the Seminole and Mexican Wars, Johnston was appointed quartermaster general of the army in 1860 but resigned to enter the Confederate service on April 22, 1861. Commissioned a brigadier general, he was placed in command of the Army of the Shenandoah at Harpers Ferry, Virginia, which was then confronting a Federal army across the Potomac River commanded by the aged Gen. Robert Patterson.[4]

The Federal Army at First Manassas, commanded by Brig. Gen. Irvin McDowell, had marched out of Arlington, Virginia, on July 16, 1861, to confront Beauregard's force with five divisions, totaling over 35,000 troops. It arrived at Fairfax Court House on July 17, about fifteen miles from Beauregard's forces along Bull Run. McDowell, a native of Columbus, Ohio, was an 1834 graduate of West Point and a veteran of the Mexican War. With none other than Secretary of the Treasury Salmon P. Chase as his patron, McDowell had been appointed a brigadier general in May 1861. Although he had never commanded any troops on a battlefield, he had been named commander of the army that protected Washington, DC. McDowell's force reached Centreville, a village consisting of nothing more than "a few houses" only four or five miles from Beauregard's defense line, on July 20.[5]

The Confederate War Department directed Johnston to bring his army to Manassas, as the real Federal threat was directed at Beauregard's positions. Accordingly, elements of General Johnston's Army of the Shenandoah, after holding General Patterson's Federal forces at bay, marched to Paris, Virginia, boarded freight trains of the Manassas Gap Railroad at Piedmont Station, and raced to Manassas Junction to reinforce Beauregard on the day before the armies clashed. Those commands arrived at Manassas Junction on the night of July 20 and the morning of July 21. Johnston arrived aboard a train accompanied by Brig. Gen. Bernard E. Bee's Fourth Alabama Infantry and right behind former Confederate congressman Col. Francis S. Bartow's Georgia and Brig. Gen. Thomas J. Jackson's Virginia brigades on July 20. As soon as Johnston's troops arrived they were led out to the growing defense lines along Bull Run. Because General Johnston was Beauregard's senior in rank, he assumed tactical command of the combined armies upon his arrival at Manassas.[6]

Beauregard's brigades had taken up positions all along the rolling heights on the west bank of Bull Run that commanded the fords of the creek. Brig. Gen. Richard S. Ewell's brigade of Alabamians was placed on the right, overlooking Union Mills Ford of Bull Run; Brig. Gen. Theophilus T. Holmes's brigade of Tennesseans and Arkansans was positioned a short distance to the rear of Ewell, and Brig. Gen. D.R. Jones's brigade was sent to the left of Ewell in front of McLean's Ford, supported then by Col. Jubal A. Early's brigade of Mississippians, South Carolinians, Virginians, and Louisianans. To the left of Jones's brigade was the North Carolina and Virginia brigade of Brig. Gen. James Longstreet at Blackburn's Ford, connecting the right of Brig. Gen. Milledge L. Bonham's brigade of North and South Carolinians. They were supported by General Jackson's brigade of Virginians from Johnston's Army of the Shenandoah. There Johnston also placed General Bee's brigade of Mississippians, Alabamians and Tennesseans, along with Colonel Bartow's small brigade of Georgians, all from the Army of the Shenandoah. Col. Philip St. George Cocke's brigade of Virginians and Louisianans, supported by Col. Arnold Elzey's brigade of Marylanders, Virginians and Tennesseans and Brig. Gen. Nathan G. "Shanks" Evans' brigade of South Carolinians and Louisianans, extended the line to the left, all the way to the stone bridge of the Warrenton Turnpike over Bull Run.[7]

Some three hundred cavalry commanded by Col. J.E.B. Stuart protected the flank and rear of Cocke's and Bonham's commands, while Col. Wade Hampton's Hampton Legion of South Carolina protected the right. Artillery, including four companies of the Washington Artillery of New Orleans, were deployed alongside the infantry regiments and along high ground, commanding the fords of Bull Run.[8]

Orders had been issued by Johnston for his troops to strike the

Federal left flank as it advanced toward Bull Run. McDowell was thinking similarly; his plan for the ensuing day was to try to turn Johnston and Beauregard's left flank.[9]

Advancing his army from Centreville toward the Confederate positions early on the morning of July 21, General McDowell directed Brig. Gen. Daniel Tyler's First Division to move along the Warrenton Turnpike toward the Confederates; its artillery batteries were directed to commence shelling the enemy guns above the fords. Col. David Hunter's Second Division followed Tyler's and, after passing a small tributary of Bull Run called Cub Run, turned right, or north, and moved around to the upper ford at the Sudley Springs Road. Hunter then turned south to turn the enemy's left flank and get to its rear. Col. Samuel P. Heintzelman's Third Division was directed to follow Hunter's and to cross Bull Run at a lower ford when and if the Confederates were driven back by Hunter's attack. Col. Dixon S. Miles' Fifth Division was held in reserve along a ridgeline west of Centreville.[10]

Hunter's advance was slowed by heat and exhaustion. The troops were raw and inexperienced; many of the troops had enlisted for only ninety days and their enlistments were to expire soon. But there were nearly 20,000 officers and men in the Federal attack force. Johnston and Beauregard responded to the movement by sending troops toward the Confederate left to meet the attack. The first to advance was Evans' brigade, which had held the stone bridge; Evans moved to a position in the fields near the intersection of the Warrenton Turnpike and the Sudley Springs Road. At the same time, McDowell ordered Heintzelman's and Tyler's divisions forward.[11]

When Hunter's Federal division reached open fields above the Warrenton Turnpike it opened fire, pushing back Evans' brigade—which had just reached the field to stem the Federal advance. The Confederate brigades of General Bee and the two Georgia regiments commanded by the gallant Colonel Bartow raced across the fields to Evans' aide, halted, and opened fire. Recalled Evans, "General Bee arrived with his brigade to my timely assistance and formed immediately in my rear, and advanced, covering and relieving my command, and was immediately hotly engaged with the enemy." Colonel Bartow, with the Eighth Georgia, a regiment he raised in Savannah, was right behind Bee. In the intense heat and high humidity, the heavy, sulphurous smoke hung close to the ground, choking the men.[12]

Though stopped by the Confederate gunfire, General Hunter's Federal attack regrouped and drove across the Warrenton Turnpike, forcing the outgunned troops of Bee, Bartow, and Evans to recoil. The commands of Generals Bee and Evans were then "completely scattered" but saved by the timely arrival of the Hampton Legion and other reinforcements. Bee reformed the commands on a long ridge to the south. There, in the smoke and confusion, he collected the Seventh and Eighth Georgia Infantry regiments of Bartow's brigade, the Fourth Alabama, Second Mississippi, and two companies of the Eleventh Mississippi regiments of his own brigade, along with a Virginia artillery battery commanded by Capt. John D. Imboden.[13]

The Federal force was just too large, and it steadily moved forward. Up the long slope of what was known as the "Spring Hill" farm the Federal attack continued, moving toward a two-story wooden-frame house of the farm's owner, the widow Judith Carter Henry. Behind that house (known as the Henry House), along a second slope, General Bee's Confederates held the line alongside General Jackson's brigade—the Second, Fourth, Fifth, Twenty-Seventh and Thirty-Third Virginia Infantry regiments.[14]

Orders were issued for Colonel Early's and Generals Holmes's and Bonham's brigades to hasten to the area. General Ewell was ordered to follow them with his brigade. Former Virginia governor Col. William F. Smith's battalion, along with Col. Eppa Hunton's Eighth Virginia Infantry, were ordered to reinforce the right. Stragglers were collected from all over the fields and ordered back into the lines. Colonel Cocke directed his men to the line on the "double-quick." Then, Brig. Gen. Edmund Kirby Smith was observed hurrying forward three regiments of Col. Arnold Elzey's brigade.[15]

Heintzelman's division, moving abreast of Hunter's, became the Federal spearhead. Cols. Orlando B. Willcox's, William B. Franklin's and Oliver Otis Howard's brigades, supported by Col. Andrew Porter's brigade of Hunter's Federal division, moved in the advance. Col. William T. Sherman's brigade of Tyler's division moved abreast of Heintzelman's and Hunter's dense masses.[16]

At the crest of the hill, south of the Henry House, Capt. James B. Ricketts's Battery I, First United States Artillery, together with Capt. Charles Griffin's Battery D, Fifth United States Artillery, unlimbered and blasted the Confederate lines. Colonel Bartow's horse was shot out from under him, and his adjutant, Lt. S.W. Branch, was killed. Bartow's Eighth Georgia Infantry suffered terribly, as did General Bee's Fourth Alabama.[17]

Nearly ten thousand Federal troops steadily moved forward; General Bee steadied his brigade and those of Evans and Bartow. He was reported to have galloped up to the flag bearer of a regiment, Capt. Porter King; Bee could not discern the unit in the smoke and asked what regiment was there. The flag bearer, holding the Stars and Bars firmly in his grasp, replied: "Don't you recognize your own men? This is all that's left of the Fourth Alabama!" It was not the first or last time in the battle that Confederates failed to distinguish their own men in the smoke and confusion. Bee's, Evans' and Bartow's men held the line alongside the five Virginia regiments commanded by General Jackson. There, General Bee, urging his men to rally alongside Jackson's Virginians, gave Jackson his famous nickname, "Stonewall." General Beauregard himself rode up to General Bee and Colonel Bartow, directing them into line on the left of Jackson's Virginians.[18]

The Confederate lines held and then attacked, driving the once-jubilant Federals back. At the head of the Seventh Georgia—and actually grasping the regiment's Stars and Bars flag—fell Colonel Bartow; he was said to have cried out to his men: "They've killed me, boys, but never give up the field." They didn't. General Bee was mortally wounded at the head of the Fourth Alabama. Some of the Federal guns near the Henry House were seized, turned around, and fired at the retreating Federals. The field was literally swept clear of Federal infantry and artillery. It had been a terrible bloodletting. Civilians who had lined the hills to view the battle with picnic baskets, including several members of Congress and their friends, were horrified at the spectacle.[19]

Most Confederate regiments at First Manassas carried variations of the Stars and Bars, state flags, or odd presentation banners. Essential in nineteenth-century warfare, regimental flags were utilized by armies to not only identify a unit but also to allow the soldiers to recognize the position of their own unit on the battlefield in the dense smoke and confusion. Battle flags were customarily carried by the color company of each regiment in the center of its battle formation so that the soldiers on either side of the flags would be able to see them. In the heavy sulphurous smoke it became difficult to tell friend from foe. Often those flags became obscured by the smoke which hung close to the ground, particularly in hot, humid weather such as at Manassas. It was found that the Confederate Stars and Bars resembled the Stars and Stripes, especially when the banner hung limp on its staff.

Col. Jubal A. Early reported an incident of mistaken identity late in the battle. Early, a native of Franklin County, Virginia, and an 1837 graduate of West Point, was a hardened veteran of the Seminole and Mexican Wars. Although he voted against secession in the Virginia Convention in 1861, he entered the Confederate army as a colonel immediately after Virginia seceded from the Union.[20]

At the time, Early was commanding a brigade in General Beauregard's Army of the Potomac. With Early on July 21 were the Seventh Virginia, the Seventh Louisiana, the Thirteenth Mississippi, and his own Twenty-Fourth Virginia Infantry regiments. The Confederates had swept the Federal troops off Henry House Hill. Early's brigade was bearing down on the fractured right flank of the Federals. In the smoke and confusion, Early turned his command to the front—where a body of Federal troops appeared on the crest of a hill, deployed as skirmishers, north of the Warrenton Turnpike and just west of the stone Matthews House and the Sudley Springs Road. It was late in the afternoon. The battlefield was covered in smoke and dust. As Early's brigade advanced on the front and flanks of the Federal force, the enemy rapidly retired behind the hill.[21]

Alongside Early's men was the hard-fighting brigade commanded by Colonel Elzey, a classmate of Early's at West Point and a veteran of the Seminole and Mexican Wars. A Marylander, Elzey entered Confederate service as colonel of the First Maryland Infantry in April 1861. That fine regiment was in Elzey's brigade that afternoon. One of Elzey's aides who had ascended the hill

The stone Matthews House facing the Warrenton Turnpike on the Manassas Battlefield. Near there Colonel Jubal A. Early mistook a Federal force for Confederates late in the battle. (Courtesy of the Library of Congress)

breathlessly relayed information that the Thirteenth Virginia Infantry was actually in front of Early's regiments, not Federal troops! Recalled Early:

> This turned out to be a misapprehension, and in the meantime a considerable body of the enemy appeared to the right of my position . . . bearing what I felt confident was the Confederate flag. It was soon, however, discovered to be a regiment of the enemy's forces.[22]

Early wrote, years after the war, that his Seventh Virginia Infantry had no flag at all, the Seventh Louisiana Infantry had a sky-blue silk flag adorned with the Pelican emblem of Louisiana, and the Thirteenth Mississippi had the Stars and Bars. "I realized that day," recalled Early, "that it was exceedingly difficult to distinguish the 'Stars and Bars' from the 'Stars and Stripes,' when both hung down around the staff."[23]

Jubal Anderson Early. (Courtesy of the Library of Congress)

Early's steadiness carried the day in spite of the mishap. Coupled with a battery of artillery and the movement of Elzey's brigade and Colonel Stuart's cavalry, Early's attack broke the Federal right flank, sending the terrified bluecoats streaming to the rear.[24]

There had been trouble identifying commands on the battlefield earlier in the day. The fighting on the Confederate right flank along Bull Run had been confusing and the smoke had been dense. A portion of Col. E.R. Burt's Eighteenth Mississippi Infantry of General Jones's brigade had moved out into a ravine only to be struck by heavy artillery and small arms fire from a Federal line in its front and the fire from other companies of Burt's own command! Burt corrected the chaotic situation without serious loss. There had been other such incidents during the fighting.[25]

Even as the battle ended there were near disasters due to the difficulty distinguishing the flags. Beauregard's adjutant general, Thomas Jordan, recalled after the war that when the battle was over he rode in advance of the Confederate lines and observed a regiment "well in advance," bearing what he was "confident must be a Federal flag, and which [he] could not believe could be [a Confederate flag] from its appearance, even when very close to it." He remembered that "it was only the appearance of the men that gave [him] confidence to approach."[26]

McDowell's Federal army, though, was soundly defeated in the bloody, day-long engagement. Its demoralized and routed troops hurried back up the Warrenton Turnpike, through Centreville and Fairfax Court House, and toward Alexandria and the defenses of Washington, DC. The ecstatic Confederates pursued McDowell's routed army all the way past Centreville, where they were halted in the evening because the troops had insufficient food and an utterly inadequate supply of ammunition and because the Federal army was still more numerous and would defend itself behind strong entrenchments in Fairfax County if attacked.[27]

More than 1,600 Federal officers and soldiers, mostly wounded, fell into the hands of the victorious Confederates. Because the Federal troops were forced back until they became disorganized—and that disorganization turned to rout—the broken Federals hastened back toward Washington, DC, leaving behind a veritable mother lode of ordnance and supplies. General Beauregard reported that the army captured twenty-eight field pieces, with over one hundred rounds of ammunition for each gun; thirty-seven caissons; six forges; four battery wagons; sixty-four artillery horses, completely equipped; 50,000 rounds of small arms ammunition; 4,500 sets of accoutrements; over 500 muskets; some nine regimental and garrison flags; a large number of pistols, knapsacks, swords, canteens, and blankets; a large store of axes and entrenching tools; wagons; ambulances; horses; camp and garrison equipage; hospital stores; and subsistence.[28]

Losses in Johnston's and Beauregard's forces amounted to 1,867: 378 killed and 1,489 wounded. McDowell's army lost many more; his casualties amounted to 481 killed, 1,011 wounded, and 1,216 missing, a total of 2,708. No American had ever seen such a bloody day up to that time.[29]

For the jubilant Confederate armies there were lessons to be learned in the great victory. Numerous times, Confederate commands had opened fire on what they believed to have been enemy forces only to discover that they were not. The need for a common battle flag for Confederate combat units became apparent. Also apparent was the need for a battle flag that was different from the Stars and Bars.

Chapter Three

"It Was an Army Affair . . . I Have Always Said So"

Generals Johnston and Beauregard pressed the Confederate pursuit of McDowell's routed Federal army as far as just east of Centreville, about six to eight miles from the Manassas battlefield. There the pursuit was halted in the darkness. The Confederate army, noted Johnston, "was more disorganized by victory than that of the United States by defeat." Some soldiers, believing they had done their duty, just left the ranks and went home; others left to attend to wounded friends in distant hospitals. The raw troops were unfit for any pursuit; few could march, much less assail entrenchments. The army needed food and ammunition— and the means of transporting them. Until August 10, recalled Johnston, the army "never had rations for more than two days, and sometimes none; nor half enough ammunition for a battle."[1]

The army established elaborate defense lines north, east, and south of Centreville, Virginia. The nearly 32,000 troops then settled into camps in the fields west and south of the village. Those camps extended for miles, even covering fields where the fighting had occurred on July 21. Until more permanent quarters could be constructed, the soldiers put up tens of thousands of tents, all arranged by companies, regiments and brigades.[2]

Johnston began reorganizing his army. Beauregard was placed in command of the First Corps. To command a second corps, Johnston named Maj. Gen. Gustavus Woodson Smith. A native of Georgetown, Kentucky, Smith was an 1842 graduate of West Point. An engineer, Smith had served in the Mexican War and then as an instructor at West Point. When the war broke out he was serving as the street commissioner of the City of New York. He was commissioned a major general in August 1861.[3]

Johnston, the army commander, moved his headquarters from "Portici"— the massive, two-story brick house of Francis W. Lewis about a mile southwest of Henry House Hill on the Manassas battlefield—to the two-story stone house at Centreville, Virginia, known as the Four Chimney House, owned by Alexander Spotswood Grigsby and his wife, Caroline, located five miles east of Johnston's battle headquarters. The Grigsby House, as the new headquarters was also known, had been used by General McDowell as his headquarters just before the fighting began at Manassas. From Centreville, Johnston would be able to oversee the troops that he had pushed forward toward Fairfax Court House in the wake of the Federal retreat.[4]

Beauregard's headquarters remained on the Manassas battlefield not far from Centreville, in the stylish, two-story brick farmhouse

Confederate winter quarters at Centreville, Virginia. In the distance is visible the Grigsby House, General Johnston's headquarters. (Courtesy of the Library of Congress)

of Wilmer McLean, his wife, Virginia, and their five children. The McLean farm was known as the Yorkshire Plantation. Beauregard always referred in correspondence to his headquarters at the McLean House as just "Manassas." Parenthetically, Wilmer McLean and his family left their Yorkshire Plantation altogether as the armies descended onto and around its fields; they moved to Appomattox Court House to get out of harm's way. McLean built a substantial two-story brick house adjacent to the Appomattox Court House. In the parlor of that house, Gen. Robert E. Lee would surrender the Army of Northern Virginia to Lt. Gen. Ulysses S. Grant on Palm Sunday, April 9, 1865![5]

Both Generals Johnston and Beauregard spent much of their time after the stunning victory over General McDowell's Federal army at Manassas reorganizing the army and desperately trying to get food, forage, and supplies to the men. Sick and wounded had to be cared for; those able to travel were sent to hospitals at Bristoe Station, five miles south of Manassas, or on to Culpeper by means of the Orange and Alexandria Railroad. Many were sent to Warrenton by means of ambulances. Ultimately, most of the

The McLean House, Gen. Beauregard's headquarters. Here is where the discussions leading up to the creation of the St. Andrew's Cross battle flag began. (Courtesy of the Library of Congress)

sick and wounded were sent to Richmond. The army needed more troops; the Federal forces were sure to renew the fighting with larger armies and better generalship. Indeed, only six days after the defeat at Manassas, President Abraham Lincoln named Maj. Gen. George B. McClellan as the commander of the newly-named Federal Army of the Potomac.[6]

But even in the midst of all the post-battle reorganization and buildup of the army—and the frantic efforts to supply it—pressure intensified for a battle flag that was distinctive and uniform for all of the regiments of the army. In late August, William Porcher Miles of South Carolina, chairman of the House Military Committee of the Provisional Confederate Congress, attempted to secure Congress's approval for a change to the Stars and Bars. Miles had been serving Beauregard as his unofficial liaison and representative in Congress. He wrote to General Beauregard on August 27, informing him of his lack of progress. Miles noted in his letter that the flag he supported had a red field with a blue cross, edged in white, with white (or gold) stars. He claimed that the flag carefully avoided the "ecclesiastical" (or Latin) cross design to which many objected. Some did not want a religious emblem on a field where men were killing one another, although many regiments and companies in the Confederate army carried banners with Christian emblems. More importantly, the Southern states had a significant Jewish population; Charleston, South Carolina, boasted of one of the largest Jewish communities of any American city. Charlestonian Charles Moise, who claimed he was a "southerner of Jewish persuasion," had written to Miles and all the members of the South Carolina Congressional Delegation requesting that "the symbol of a particular religion" not be incorporated into the emblems of the new Confederacy. Miles noted to Beauregard that his flag contained the "saltire" of heraldry, a symbol of "strength" and "progress." Miles then concluded:

> But I am boring you with my pet hobby in the matter of the flag. I wish sincerely Congress would change the present one. Your reasons are conclusive in my mind. But I fear it is just as hard now as it was at Montgomery to tear people away entirely from the desire to appropriate some reminiscence of the old [United States] flag.[7]

Beauregard was very concerned about the lack of a distinctive and uniform battle flag for the regiments of the army. Time was of the essence to him. Miles had introduced Beauregard to a design, though, that would soon become the single-most iconic of all flags of the Confederacy—and, perhaps, of the American Civil War.

The next day, August 28, 1861, Miles offered a resolution in Congress to inquire into a more distinctive flag. The resolution was adopted, but the House Military Committee refused to agree to a change of the flag in accord with Miles' design. Miles quickly scribbled a note to Beauregard about his lack of progress.[8]

Impressed with Miles' design as an army battle flag, and recognizing the Confederate Congress was not going to do anything, Beauregard proposed to adopt the design in a letter he wrote to Miles from the McLean House at "Manassas" on September 4, 1861, as a military necessity. Beauregard wrote:

I regret to hear of the failure about the change of flag; but what can now be done is to authorize commanding generals in the field to furnish their troops with a 'field, or battle flag,' which shall be according to your design, leaving out, however, the white border, or rim, separating the blue from the red. I would have it simply a red ground with two blue bars crossing each other diagonally, on which shall be the white stars; white or golden fringe might go all around the sides of the flag; we would then have two flags—peace, or parade, flag, and a war flag. This would obviate all difficulties.[9]

Beauregard broached his idea the next day—September 5, 1861—in a letter to Gen. Joseph E. Johnston at the Grigsby House at Centreville. From his headquarters, which he designated as "Manassas," Beauregard wrote:

Colonel [William Porcher] Miles informs me that the flag committee voted down any change of our flag by a vote of four to one, he being alone in favor of it. I wrote to him then to propose that we should have two flags—a peace or parade flag, and a war flag, to be used only on the field of battle—but Congress having adjourned, no action will be taken in the matter. How would it do for us to address the War Department on the subject for a supply of regimental war, or badge flags, made of red with two bars crossing each other diagonally, on which shall be introduced the stars—the edge of the flag to be trimmed all around with white, yellow, or

William Porcher Miles of South Carolina, the earliest advocate of the St. Andrew's Cross as a battle flag and the one who convinced General Beauregard to adopt it. (Courtesy of the Library of Congress)

General P.G.T. Beauregard. It was Beauregard who first advocated a distinct battle flag, and urged the use of the St. Andrew's Cross. (Courtesy of the Library of Congress)

gold fringe? We would then, on the field of battle, know our friends from our enemies.[10]

Having considerable interest in the subject himself, General Johnston welcomed the proposal. Because of the "difficulty of distinguishing the colors of the armies from each other," he wrote, he had "attempted to procure, from the different southern states, state flags for their regiments." He had learned thereafter that the Virginia regiments were to be supplied with state flags by direction of Gov. John Letcher; none of the regiments from the other Confederate states, however, were going to be provided with state banners any time soon. Johnston believed the need for a uniform and distinctive battle flag for his army was absolutely necessary—and urgent.[11]

Never did Johnston agree, or even respond in writing, to Beauregard's inquiry about "address[ing] the War Department." Even in the infant Confederacy, Johnston realized that the bureaucracy of the War Department would likely kill any attempt to secure a change of the flag by time-consuming interdepartmental referrals, complete inaction, or dilatory deference to Congress. An inquiry would only wind up prohibiting any effort to speedily get battle flags the army could use, as asking would make it difficult to unilaterally order them produced without first obtaining an answer, and a denial would foreclose any other effort. Any long, drawn-out process would defeat the purpose. Johnston undoubtedly believed he should act on his own in the best interest of the army.

A conference was called most likely at Beauregard's "Manassas" headquarters, behind the extensive Centreville camps and overlooking Bull Run. The initial conference would have taken place close to September 5, 1861, the date of Beauregard's letter to Johnston, which would have been delivered that day. The matter was important to both Beauregard and Johnston. Undoubtedly, the first conference where a change of the flag was discussed would have taken place before September 12, the date the army moved to Fairfax Court House. That conference would not have been called just for purposes of discussing the flag, but the flag question would have arisen along with many other matters of

General Joseph E. Johnston. It was Johnston who finally directed the creation and the issuing of the first St. Andrew's Cross battle flags to the regiments of the army. (Courtesy of the Library of Congress)

military importance. The principal officer in charge of overseeing the making of the flags, Lt. Colin McRae Selph, recalled that the question of the change of the flag was "under advisement from Bull Run to Fairfax Court House." Wherever Selph meant Centreville or Fairfax Court House in his correspondence, he named the site explicitly. He was very exact. Here, he used "Bull Run," the site of Beauregard's headquarters, as the site where the discussion began. The impetus to adopt a new battle flag for the army clearly started at "Bull Run."[12]

At any initial conference, General Beauregard (commander of the First Corps of the Army of the Potomac), General Johnston (the army commander), General Smith (commander of the Second Corps, which included the brigades of Johnston's former Army of the Shenandoah), and their staff officers would have been present. Those generals and their staffs conducted many conferences in and around the Centreville camps about new intelligence about the enemy, the troops under their command, the supply of the army, and any movement the army needed to embark upon, offensively or defensively. The generals were also about to move the army forward to Fairfax Court House, necessitating immense coordination and consultation.[13]

There must have been some opening banter among the officers gathered at Beauregard's headquarters as the McLean House had suffered damage during the fighting at Manassas. It seems that on July 18, as Federal forces were massed along Mitchell's and Blackburn's Fords on the east bank of Bull Run, they endeavored to force a passage at Blackburn's Ford not far from the McLean House. General Longstreet's forces, aided by Colonel Early's brigade, repulsed the Federal advance. The whole affair, however, "lapsed into an artillery duel" between Federal batteries and none other than the Washington Artillery of New Orleans, the guns of which overlooked and commanded McLean's, Blackburn's, and Union Mills Fords of Bull Run. As General Beauregard and his staff sat down to dinner that day, a Federal shell hit the dining room fireplace, destroying the meal and sending rocks, bricks, splinters, and furnishings—along with the general and his staff officers—flying in all directions. The effects of the shell explosion were plainly visible to all at the conference.[14]

Johnston, Beauregard, and Smith got down to business; there was much to discuss and the flag question was just one of many matters of importance. Beauregard recalled that he submitted his views about the design of the flag. Considered also was the Latin cross design of Edward C. Hancock of New Orleans, advocated by Maj. James Burdge Walton of the Washington Artillery of New Orleans, although he was probably not at the conference. Walton, a forty-eight-year-old native of Newark, New Jersey, who attended the University of Louisiana (a forerunner of Tulane University), was a well-known auctioneer in New Orleans when the war broke out. A veteran of the Mexican War, Walton was the adjutant of the Washington Artillery Battalion when it was formed in 1839. He was the major of the battalion when it was accepted into Confederate service in May 1861. It was Walton's guns that had been positioned in the McLean fields when Beauregard's headquarters at the McLean House was hit by the Federal shell. Walton was well-known among the high command of the army as an advocate for a change of the flag; he had presented his ideas to William Porcher Miles, and Miles had undoubtedly discussed those ideas with Beauregard. All of the flag designs discussed by those in attendance at the conference called for the banners to be "oblong," or rectangular. Johnston listened to all proposals and took the matter under advisement. The conference did not conclude with a decision about the change of the flag![15]

After multiple conferences with his generals, Johnston moved his army to Fairfax Court House, ten miles east of Centreville, on September 12, 1861. Strong cavalry outposts were sent out to occupy Munson's Hill (in Fairfax County) and Mason's Hill (at the border of Fairfax and Arlington Counties), with cavalry protecting the flanks. While holding the lines near Fairfax Court House, Johnston's army was reorganized into four divisions; newly-minted Maj. Gens. Earl Van Dorn, Gustavus Woodson Smith, James Longstreet, and Thomas J. "Stonewall" Jackson were named commanders. The Federal army, growing in size every day, held entrenchments and gun emplacements that covered a front from a point on the Virginia side of the Potomac River above Georgetown all the way to the hills south of Alexandria.[16]

Throughout the time the army was at Fairfax Court House,

the creation of a uniform flag for the army remained under discussion. There were multiple conferences at Fairfax Court House. Those conferences mostly included Gens. Johnston, Beauregard, and Smith. Insofar as the question of changing the flag was concerned, nothing was decided at Fairfax Court House. Beauregard remembered that he oversaw the preparation of "colored drawings" of the battle flag he advocated on a "simple board," which he submitted to Johnston at Fairfax Court House after the army moved there, but they were not handed to Johnston at any conference called to discuss the matter. Johnston later acknowledged that he "had no conference with the War Department or [any] civilians" about the design of the flag or the making of 120 such flags. If a change of flag was to be ordered, it would be given by him without consultation with anyone outside of the army. That change would be ordered as a military necessity.[17]

By about September 20, 1861, Johnston became convinced that the increasing size and strength of the Federal army made his positions at Fairfax Court House hazardous. The cavalry outposts at Munson's and Mason's Hills were withdrawn first. The entire army was ordered back to Centreville, a place Johnston referred to years after the war as giving his army a "stronger . . . front, as well as [a position] less easily and safely turned." There, on October 19, Johnston concentrated his troops; he directed his army to set about building winter quarters in Centreville and along the Centreville Plateau between Little Rocky Run and Bull Run. Johnston, as army commander, would have arrived at Centreville days before the entire army completed its movement.[18]

It was only as Johnston's army returned to Centreville that a decision was made by General Johnston about obtaining uniform battle flags for the army that were different from the Stars and Bars. Recalled Lt. Selph: "General Johnston did not adopt [any pattern flag] until our headquarters were moved [back to] Centreville." When Johnston made his decision, he called his chief quartermaster, Maj. William L. Cabell, to army headquarters. Major Cabell met with Johnson at the Grigsby House days before October 19, 1861. A native of Danville, Virginia, Cabell was an 1850

Maj. William Lewis Cabell, chief quartermaster of the Confederate Army of the Potomac, a sketch made during the war. (Courtesy of the Museum of the Confederacy, Richmond, Virginia. Photography by Alan Thompson)

graduate of West Point. Thirty-four years old, he had seen service almost exclusively in the quartermaster department of the United States Army before resigning his commission in 1861. He would later be transferred to the Trans-Mississippi theater under Gen. Earl Van Dorn; there he would be elevated to the rank of brigadier general in 1863. Being the army quartermaster, Cabell would be required to assemble the necessary people and material to make the flags. The quartermaster department also controlled the army's money that would be needed to purchase the materials. Thus, when Johnston called Cabell to his headquarters it was for the purpose of giving Cabell orders to produce the flags.[19]

As the army was settling into camps around Centreville, General Johnston announced his decision to his quartermaster at the Grigsby House. The matter had been under consideration by him since the conference at Beauregard's headquarters overlooking Bull Run, nearly three weeks before.[20]

Recalled General Johnston after the war: "I selected one of those [designs Beauregard] offered, but changed the shape to square, and fixed the size; . . . colors of infantry to be four feet, . . . artillery three [feet] and cavalry . . . two and a half [feet]." Square flags, reasoned Johnston, were easier to carry than "oblong" ones. Because the artillery and cavalry arms of the service necessitated standard bearers to be mounted, square flags, smaller in size than those carried by infantry regiments, were deemed necessary by

The Grigsby House, Centreville, Virginia, General Johnston's headquarters. There General Johnston ordered the St. Andrew's Cross battle flags to be made and issued to the army. (Courtesy of the Library of Congress)

Johnston for ease in carrying. Johnston then called upon Major Cabell and his quartermaster department of the army to make the flags for each regiment in the army, 120 in all.[21]

Generals Johnston and Beauregard had literally determined to bypass Congress and the War Department and, on their own, create and issue battle flags that were distinctive and uniform, as a military necessity. After the war, Johnston wrote: "My recollection is that it was an army affair, and when questioned on the subject, I have always said so."[22]

Chapter Four

"[I] First Solicited the Assistance of Mrs. James Alfred Jones"

Selected to oversee the making of the battle flags was young Lt. Colin McRae Selph, an aide to chief army quartermaster Maj. William L. Cabell. Twenty-two-year-old Selph was born in December 1839 in Mississippi City, Mississippi. At an early age he attended a military academy at Staunton, Virginia, and then entered the University of Virginia at Charlottesville. He graduated from the law school at the University of Virginia with high honors. Immediately thereafter, he became a member of the bar of the State of Louisiana. After a tour of Europe, he returned to Mississippi but later journeyed to New Orleans, where he entered the practice of law. Just before the Civil War broke out, he enlisted in the Washington Artillery of New Orleans and was commissioned a lieutenant. He married the former Elizabeth Dimitry on March 16, 1861. As the first four companies of the Washington Artillery were transferred to Virginia, Selph accompanied them; once in Richmond, he was assigned to the quartermaster department of Quartermaster General Abraham C. Myers as an assistant quartermaster on May 3. Selph served in Richmond until he was assigned to the staff of Major Cabell at Manassas, an assignment that was dated July 27, 1861. Unquestionably, Selph was selected by Major Cabell to oversee the making of the battle flags because he had served in the quartermaster department in Richmond for nearly three months; he was familiar with the quartermaster general and his staff and was familiar with Richmond and many of the people in that city.[1]

Cabell told Selph that the army needed 120 battle flags.

Lieutenant Selph was given Beauregard's watercolor drawings of the proposed battle flag by Major Cabell; Selph was also given a requisition for sufficient money to purchase the silk to be given to Confederate Quartermaster General Myers in Richmond, on whose staff Selph had served before reporting to Manassas. Myers was of a prominent Jewish family from Charleston, South Carolina; his great-grandfather was the hazzan of Charleston's Beth Elohim congregation. He was an 1833 graduate of West Point and a veteran of the Seminole and Mexican Wars. Lieutenant Selph recalled that General Myers not only supplied the money, but also went so far as to write an "eloquent appeal" to those individuals Selph would approach to make the flags.[2]

Selph took the money and went to dry goods and clothing stores and wholesalers in Richmond to acquire the necessary silk. A city of more than 37,000 people, Richmond boasted sixty retail clothing stores, multiple second-hand-clothing businesses, and two wholesale clothing dealers. Probably the most popular store for ladies' silks was Keen, Baldwin & Williams Clothiers at 162 Main Street. Selph very likely went to Keen, Baldwin & Williams to acquire some or all of the silk he needed. There were four retail shops where trimmings and gold fringe could be obtained. All but one were located on Broad Street between Fourth and Sixth Streets; the other was on Main Street.[3]

Selph purchased red, white, and blue silk material. The red silk strips were actually variations of that color. Some were rose, others were pink; most of them were from bolts at least 16½ inches wide. Cut from bolts of similar width, the blue silk was almost uniformly a dark marine blue. It seemed to be resolved early on to apply the five-pointed stars to the flags by means of gold paint. There were shops in Richmond that could perform that work. Edward T. Finch at 184 Main Street was a "chemist;" he may have been the one with whom Selph contracted. There were also three "artists," two on Broad Street and the other on Marshall Street, between Third and Fourth Streets.[4]

Selph recalled: "I bought the silk, red, blue and white (red of all tints, magenta, solferino, pink, etc.) [at Richmond, Virginia] and first solicited the assistance of Mrs. James Alfred Jones, the wife of one of Virginia's most distinguished jurists." The woman Selph chose to stitch together the first St. Andrew's Cross battle flag was the beautiful, twenty-eight-year-old, dark-haired, former Mary Henry Lyon. The daughter of James Gaines Lyon and Lavinia C. Lyon of Mobile, Alabama, Mary was born on November 12, 1833. It was written almost prophetically that she was "ushered into life" during a night marked by a "shower" of falling stars. Orphaned early in her life, Mary had lived at beautiful "Bluff Hall" overlooking the Tombigbee River in Demopolis, Alabama, with her uncle and guardian, Francis Strother Lyon. Bluff Hall was a sprawling two-story, white-washed brick, Greek revival mansion that literally stood atop the imposing bluffs above the river.[5]

Mary's uncle and guardian had been born on February 25, 1800, in Stokes County, North Carolina, the son of James Lyon and Behethland Gaines Lyon. He moved to Marengo County, Alabama, in 1817 to live with his uncle, Col. George Strother Gaines. Admitted to the bar in 1821, Francis Strother Lyon served as secretary of the Alabama State Senate from 1822 to 1830 before he himself was elected as a state senator, serving from 1833 to 1844. (He was also elected to represent Alabama's Fifth Congressional District in the United States House of Representatives from 1835 to 1839.) Serving in the Alabama House of Representatives at the outbreak of the Civil War, Lyon would be elected to represent the state in the First and the Second Confederate Congresses from 1862 to 1865. Mary would often address Francis Strother Lyon in letters as "my dearest parent" and sign them below the words "your affectionate child."[6]

Mary Henry Lyon won the affections of many. She attended a boarding school in New Haven, Connecticut. "I can never forget her," wrote a schoolmate, "as I first saw her in her youthful beauty, when she came up to console me, a very homesick, awkward school girl. I loved her on the spot, and I've loved her ever since. I think she was the best loved woman I ever knew, and no wonder."[7]

On June 30, 1858, Mary Henry Lyon married James Alfred Jones in Mobile. They probably met while James was visiting his older brother, Robert Tignall Jones. Robert was an 1837 graduate of West Point who had resigned his commission in the United States Army in 1838 and moved to Perry County, Alabama, where he became a planter and president of the Cahaba, Marion and Greensborough Railroad. He married twice; both of his wives were natives of Perry County. Robert's home was not more than twenty miles from Demopolis, where Mary was living at the time. Mary was thirteen years younger than James.[8]

The son of James B. Jones and Judith Bailey Hall Jones of Mecklenburg County, Virginia, James Alfred Jones was born in that county on June 3, 1820. He was a collateral descendant of the great judge and legal scholar, Littleton Waller Tazewell. James graduated from the University of Virginia with a master of arts degree at the age of nineteen. Thereafter, he received an LLD degree from Richmond College. James had commenced the study of law under the guidance of a lawyer named Conway Robinson in Richmond, Virginia, and was licensed to practice law in the capital city in July 1840. James first settled in Petersburg, Virginia, where he was elected to the 1851 Constitutional Convention—to which he vigorously objected—and to the State Senate in 1853. He moved back to Richmond in 1857 and entered into a law practice with Conway Robinson; their offices were located on Franklin Street, between Eleventh and Twelfth Streets, just below the Virginia state capitol.[9]

James Alfred Jones was described by a contemporary as "learned in the laws [with] an extensive reputation as a sound lawyer; [he was] a logical and concise legal debater." An ardent advocate of states' rights, it was written that he "steadily adhered to [that doctrine] throughout his life." For all his appearances as a hard-nosed lawyer, James was thoroughly in love with Mary. When they were apart, he would write Mary long, newsy letters, which he would end with the words "truly devoted," or "ever your devoted husband" above his signature.[10]

Mary Henry Lyon Jones moved to Richmond, Virginia, with her husband, settling in a substantial brick house on 15 North Sixth Street, between Franklin and Main Streets. In Richmond, James had a very active law practice, and there the couple became active parishioners of St. James Episcopal Church, which stood at the corner of Fifth and Marshall Streets not far from the Jones's home.[11]

Col. Robert T. Jones of the Twelfth Alabama Infantry, brother of James Alfred Jones. Colonel Jones was killed at the Battle of Seven Pines on May 31, 1862. (Courtesy of the Alabama Department of Archives and History, Montgomery, Alabama)

Richmond, Virginia, looking toward the area of the city where Mary Henry Lyon Jones lived (beyond the steeple in the center of the photograph). (Courtesy of the Library of Congress)

How and why Lieutenant Selph selected Mary was never discussed or related by him afterwards; it may be lost to history, but maybe not. The quartermaster's service was designated by Confederate army regulations as the department that oversaw not only the acquisition, maintenance, and requisition of equipment, wagons, horses and mules, clothing, and forage for the army, but also all of the army's ambulances, medicals, medical instruments, and litters; it was also the duty of the quartermaster department to set up and maintain all hospitals. After the Battle of Manassas, sick and wounded poured into Richmond, many by means of the Richmond, Fredericksburg and Potomac Railroad—which then extended only from Richmond to Aquia Creek, twenty miles south of Manassas Junction—and the Virginia Central Railroad, which connected with the Orange and Alexandria Railroad at Gordonsville. The Orange and Alexandria brought the sick and wounded from Manassas Junction, Bristoe Station, and Culpeper, all towns connected to Gordonsville by that railroad. Others were brought to Richmond by ambulances and a multitude of other conveyances from a host of other hospitals behind Johnston's and Beauregard's lines.[12]

The quartermaster department established numerous military hospitals throughout the city. There would be near fifty such hospitals in Richmond by the end of the fall of 1861. By October 2 of that year, ladies groups in Richmond had established sixteen hospitals. Many of the ladies' hospitals were established by the Ladies' Aid Society and church groups, and were scattered all over the city; most of them, though, were between Third and Ninth Streets on Clay, Cary, Main and Franklin Streets.[13]

One of the most remarkable ladies' hospitals was established in a lovely two-story, whitewashed, wooden-frame house at the corner of Main and Third Streets. The house was owned by Judge John Robertson, who had moved his family out of the city. In the wake of the casualties pouring into Richmond, twenty-seven-year-old Miss Sally Louisa Tompkins, who had been left with a sizeable inheritance, wanted to open a hospital. Judge Robertson agreed to let Sally use his house as long as there was a need for it. Sally approached the ladies of her church, St. James Episcopal, to help her. Between July 21 and 30, Sally and the ladies of her church worked around the clock, setting up Judge Robertson's house to receive wounded. As early as July 30, only nine days after the Battle of Manassas, Sally Tompkins and the ladies of St. James Church opened the Robertson house as a hospital. Sally had even employed Dr. A.Y.P. Garnett as chief surgeon; Garnett had recently moved to Richmond from Washington, DC.[14]

One of the ladies who helped Sally set up Robertson Hospital was Mary Henry Lyon Jones, who lived only two half-blocks east. Mary had attended primarily to sick soldiers in military and ladies' hospitals on and off throughout the summer. But, as the wounded poured into the city after the fighting at Manassas, she assisted Sally in setting up and operating what became known as Robertson Hospital on nearly a daily basis. A North Carolina soldier even commented in his local newspaper about the care given to him by "Miss Sally Tompkins" and the "lady living a few doors from the [hospital]," very possibly a reference to Mary. On October 5, 1861, more than sixty days after the hospital had opened, the *Richmond Enquirer* finally reported that "the ladies connected with St. James Church have established a hospital at the corner of Main and Third Streets for our wounded soldiers."

Mary was spotted there eight days later by none other than diarist Mary Boykin Chesnut of South Carolina; Mary Henry Lyon Jones was an attendant that day with Martha Milledge Flournoy Carter, formerly of Augusta, Georgia, and a communicant at St. James. Chesnut recorded five visits to Robertson Hospital that fall.[15]

Lieutenant Selph unquestionably became acquainted with Mary while he was serving as an assistant quartermaster overseeing the establishment of the hospitals in Richmond. He probably helped Sally and her church ladies set up Robertson Hospital; he certainly aided them in obtaining litters, medicals, medical instruments, and bandage rolls. He also helped forward patients to the hospital. Selph must have liked Mary from the start; she was attractive and hardworking. He departed for Manassas in early August 1861 knowing where Mary lived and where she could be found. Mary was also an ardent Confederate; her uncle would soon be elected to the Confederate Congress and her brother, Lt. William Dunn Lyon of the First Alabama Battalion, would soon join the staff of none other than Gen. Joseph E. Johnston at Centreville.[16]

Given rose, white, and dark blue silk by Lieutenant Selph, Mary Henry Lyon Jones stitched a flag following Beauregard's watercolor sketches that were also given to her by Selph. The flag she made was 30 inches square. The field was made from two pieces of rose-colored silk. The saltire was dark blue, 5⅛ inches wide with a white edge, ½ inch wide. Twelve five-pointed stars, three on each of the four arms of the saltire, were painted on in gold by a chemist or artists in Richmond. The stars were 2¾ inches in diameter and placed just under four inches apart. There was no star in the center of the cross. The white border of the flag was 1⅞ inches wide. The border along the leading edge was doubled and sewn; it had four whipped eyelets to attach the flag to a staff. It took Mary just under one week to complete the flag.[17]

When Mary completed the flag, Lieutenant Selph returned and took it back to General Johnston for his approval on October 21, 1861. Johnston, most likely after consulting with General Beauregard and Major Cabell, approved it; Johnston instructed Selph to immediately return to Richmond and complete the production of the rest of the flags. Selph approached Mary and other women, including the Richmond Ladies' Aid Society, asking

Colin McRae Selph, a photograph taken in New Orleans after the war. It was Selph who organized the ladies groups in Richmond and oversaw the making of the battle flags. (Courtesy of LHAP, T-HML, TU)

them to collect their members, friends, relatives, and those from their church groups and altar guilds, and produce the necessary number of flags for the army.[18]

It is easy to understand why Lieutenant Selph chose to use women's groups to make the flags. The effort would require a large number of individuals with great skills, working almost constantly over a very long period of time, maybe four weeks. Use of commercial enterprises would be inadequate, as not enough skilled individuals could be brought to the task for that long period of time. Also, Selph had seen the women of Richmond while he was a quartermaster there during the summer. They were hardworking and focused; whatever they produced was always of high quality. They also were highly organized in large groups, mostly by the Ladies' Aid Society and churches. The use of commercial enterprises probably would have cost more than the quartermaster department had authorized. The final determinant for Selph was secrecy. To give the work to commercial enterprises would guarantee that the project would become known all over the city within hours of its beginning. The effort was not authorized by the War Department, and Selph had no idea how the government would respond if the news of it was widely broadcast. The project might be shut down. If there was any hope of keeping the project quiet—and getting it accomplished within thirty days— the use of women's groups was essential.

Mary Henry Lyon Jones gathered a group of ladies in her Richmond home that included Mary Foote, daughter of cotton factor and banker Charles King Foote of Mobile, Alabama. Foote's wife was none other than Sarah Behethland Lyon Foote, the elder half sister of Mary Henry Lyon Jones. Another lady in the group was James's niece, Mary Jones, daughter of none other than James's brother, Col. Robert Tignall Jones, who had become commander of the Twelfth Alabama Infantry in 1861 and who was then at Centreville. He would be killed at the Battle of Seven Pines on May 31, 1862, at the age of fifty-seven. Also there was Addie Deane, daughter of Dr. Francis H. Deane of Richmond. There were many others; all of them were either family members or women from St. James Episcopal Church.[19]

Other groups of Richmond women were formed by the Ladies'

Aid Society and by at least four other churches. Some of the
ladies gathered around the famed Cary girls, who were also asked
by Lieutenant Selph to help make the necessary flags. One of the
Cary girls was eighteen-year-old-Constance Fairfax Cary, a native
of Port Gibson, Mississippi; she had blue eyes and auburn hair.
Born on April 25, 1843, to Archibald Cary and Monimia Fairfax
Cary, Constance grew up in Cumberland, Maryland, living there
until her father died in 1854. She then moved to "Vaucluse," the
Fairfax County, Virginia, plantation of her maternal grandmother
that was located near the Episcopal Theological Seminary of
Virginia outside of Alexandria. Constance was a direct descendant
of none other than Thomas, the ninth Lord Fairfax, whose
extensive properties included much of northern Virginia and the
Northern Neck of the State.[20]

Constance refugeed from "Vaucluse" with her mother in the
early summer of 1861 after Federal forces moved closer to the
Confederate lines than they did in Fairfax County prior to the Battle
of Manassas. Some Federal fortifications of the defenses of the City
of Washington, DC, were actually constructed on the "Vaucluse"
properties; the lovely gothic revival house of the Fairfax family was
burned to the ground and all of its woodlots were cut down, "a
sacrifice by the [Federal] troops," recalled Constance.[21]

Constance and her mother took refuge first at the Confederate
army's camps in Fairfax County before the Battle of Manassas.
Just prior to the fighting at Manassas, they were sent to Bristoe
Station, four miles south of Manassas Junction on the Orange and
Alexandria Railroad, where they stayed at the railroad hotel next
to the tracks. There they nursed Confederate sick and wounded
during and after the Battle of Manassas. They were then sent to
nurse sick and wounded Confederates at Culpeper, thirty-three
miles down the tracks of the Orange and Alexandria from Bristoe
Station. They cared for the sick at the Methodist hospital and then
treated the wounded both at that site and the receiving hospital
set up by the army. Constance returned to Fairfax County when
the Confederate army advanced there in early September 1861.[22]

It was in the Confederate camps near Fairfax Court House
before the Battle of Manassas that Constance came upon her first
cousins, Hetty and Jennie Cary of Baltimore, Maryland. Born at

"Haystacks," the family farm house, outside of Baltimore, Hetty Carr Cary and Jane "Jennie" Margaret Cary were the daughters of Wilson Miles Cary—the brother of Constance Cary's father, Archibald Cary—and the former Jane Margaret Carr. By the outbreak of the Civil War, the Carys resided in a row house on Eutaw Street at the corner of Biddle Street in Baltimore. The family had suffered financial reversals, forcing the sale of their farm; Jane Carr ran a dame school in their home to help with family expenses. Hetty and Jennie's paternal grandfather, Wilson Jefferson Cary, was a nephew of Thomas Jefferson. He married Virginia Randolph of Tuckahoe plantation, Goochland County, Virginia, in a wedding that took place on August 28, 1805, at Monticello, Jefferson's magnificent home in Albemarle County (near Charlottesville). William Jefferson Cary is buried at Monticello. Hetty and Jennie's mother was also a collateral descendant of Jefferson; their maternal great-grandmother was none other than Martha Jefferson, the president's sister. Martha Jefferson married Dabney Carr, one of Jefferson's closest friends. Dabney Carr and his wife are actually buried in the Jefferson Cemetery at Monticello. Hetty and Jennie Cary—and their first cousin Constance—were thus true "members" of the first families of the Old Dominion. Hetty and Jennie would journey to Charlottesville often to visit with all of their numerous family members who resided there in the shadow of Jefferson's Monticello.[23]

Twenty-five-year-old, blue-eyed Hetty was described by Marylander Henry Kyd Douglas, one of Gen. Thomas J. "Stonewall" Jackson's staff officers, as "the most beautiful woman of her day and generation." Douglas went even further, claiming Hetty was "the handsomest woman in the Southland—with her classic face, her pure complexion, her auburn hair, her perfect figure and her courage, altogether the most beautiful woman I ever saw in any land." Hetty's sister, Jennie, eighteen years old, and with auburn hair and blue eyes, was less striking than Hetty, but, for all that can be discerned, she was popular and held her own in any and all company.[24]

The Cary sisters were refugees, having been forced to leave Baltimore by Federal authorities because of their tireless efforts to make uniforms and collect medicals and supplies for shipment to the Marylanders fighting for the Confederacy in Virginia. They actually organized a group of women in Baltimore to assist them. The group was named the Monument Street Girls.[25]

Events spun out of control on April 19, 1861, when a mob met the Sixth Massachusetts Infantry in Baltimore on its way to take a train to Washington, DC. A riot ensued; four soldiers and twelve civilians were killed. Then came martial law. The Carys soon learned of the arrest of their cousin and Confederate sympathizer, Francis Key Howard, the editor of the *Baltimore Sun*, by Federal authorities. Howard was the grandson of none other than Francis Scott Key, who wrote the "Star Spangled Banner" while watching the bombardment of Fort McHenry as a prisoner of war on a British vessel. In a touch of irony, Francis Key Howard was imprisoned by the Federal authorities in Fort McHenry. Other secessionists, many of whom were lawmakers and city administrators, were arrested in the same "reign of terror" that caught Howard.

It was probably Jennie Cary who set the words of the poem "Maryland, My Maryland" to the tune of "O, Tannenbaum." She discovered the nine-stanza poem after it was published in a Baltimore newspaper by James Ryder Randall, the poet. The poem described the "depression beneath the despot's heel." Jennie sang the song in defiance of Federal soldiers who gathered near her house. Not to be outdone, Hetty Cary waved a Confederate flag from the balcony of her Eutaw Street house to the anger of the Federal troops. When one soldier asked his commander if he should arrest her, his colonel replied: "No, she is beautiful enough to do as she . . . pleases."[26]

To avoid arrest by Federal forces—which was inevitable given their adamancy for the Confederate cause—Hetty and Jennie Cary crossed the Potomac River and landed in Westmoreland County, Virginia, on July 4, 1861. The Cary girls first found their way to Orange Court House, Virginia, a lovely town on the Orange and Alexandria Railroad located twenty miles southwest of Culpeper and seventy-three miles southwest of Fairfax Station. At Orange Court House the Carys stayed with friends, the family of Dr. Thomas T. Slaughter, a prominent physician. They wound up behind the Confederate army at Fairfax Station before the clash at Manassas.[27]

The Cary girls seemed to be everywhere. It was said they arrived at Fairfax Station riding on the cow catcher of a locomotive to the cheers of everyone there. They quickly had an entrée to General Beauregard's headquarters. Constance Cary recalled that she and her two cousins were at Beauregard's headquarters when "the lamented" former Confederate congressman Col. Francis S. Bartow of Georgia arrived to be greeted by them. Gen. James Longstreet was a favorite of the Carys; in the days before the general lost several of his children to scarlet fever, Constance found him "rollicking and jolly always."[28]

An incident was related after the war by Col. G. Moxley Sorrel of General Longstreet's staff that illustrates how admired the Cary girls were, particularly Hetty. The three Cary girls appeared in the camps of General Elzey's brigade at Fairfax Station. After spending considerable time talking and having refreshments with Elzey and his staff, the girls were escorted to the camp's parade ground. There, Col. George H. Steuart of the First Maryland Infantry had his regiment in line. Steuart insisted that the girls take a position alongside him. As the regiment went through the manual of arms, Colonel Steuart handed his sword to Hetty and stepped back, leaving her alone in command of the regiment. "Thus," recalled Sorrel, "the regiment, amid much enthusiasm, was put through its manual by the prettiest woman in Virginia."[29]

After the Battle of Manassas, the Cary girls returned to the army. They were provided a tent and even guards. It is likely that General Beauregard aided and provided them with quarters not far from his own headquarters. Recalled Constance: "[The three girls] slept, or rather giggled, half the night, upon layers of cartridge flannel on the hard floor of a tent, with a row of hoop-skirts hanging like balloons on the pole overhead, and soldiers guarding us outside." So visible and popular were they that the Cary girls were even invited to dine with Beauregard; the supper that evening consisted of what Beauregard described as his "last duck."[30]

It was on the occasion of that dinner at Beauregard's headquarters that the three Cary girls organized the "Cary Invincibles." Those who were "commissioned" or given lesser positions in the Cary girls' "command" illustrate the incredible company they kept. The Cary Invincibles represented a who's who in the Confederate Army of the Potomac. Constance was "commissioned" "captain-general," Hetty, "lieutenant colonel," and Jennie, "first lieutenant." Many dignitaries were placed in "inferior positions," recalled Constance. Maj. Alfred M. Barbour, chief quartermaster to General Bonham and, probably, Major Albert S. Van De Graaff, who attended Yale University and the University of Virginia and then was serving in the Fifth Alabama Battalion, were named "military engineers;" Lt. William Waters Boyce, a congressman from South Carolina, and Lt. Philip Beverly Hooe, of the Seventeenth Virginia Infantry, were "commissioned" "staff officers;" Lt. Col. William Munford of the Seventeenth Virginia Infantry was made "historian and bard;" the Hon. Mr. Thomas Lanier Clingman, the former United States senator from North Carolina and colonel of the Twenty-Fifth North Carolina Infantry, was named "private secretary;" a Mr. John Addison became "chief cook;" former governor John Lawrence Manning of South Carolina was named "scribe general;" and the *vivandiere* was Maj. Andrew Dewees Banks, a volunteer aide to Gen. Smith Banks who had been a newspaper editor in Petersburg, Virginia, (with the Confederate congressman Roger A. Pryor) and then a Washington, DC, correspondent to the *Cincinnati Enquirer* before the war. It seems Major Barbour and Major Banks were brought into the group by another aid to General Bonham, Wilson Miles Cary, the twenty-three-year-old brother of Hetty and Jennie Cary.[31]

When all the Cary girls finally arrived in Richmond with Constance's mother, they dined, it was said, at none other than Robert E. Lee's table at the Spotswood Hotel at the corner of Main and Eighth Streets. They took up residence in the city, most likely at that hotel; Constance's mother served as their chaperone. Eventually, all the Carys took up residence in a boarding house on Franklin Street.[32]

Captain Selph recalled taking the flag Mary Henry Lyon Jones had made and handing it to Constance Cary as a guide for her and her cousins to follow. Selph gave the Cary girls sufficient money from the quartermaster general to purchase the necessary material from the retailers and wholesalers in the city.[33]

Representing church groups and altar guilds from no fewer than five churches—including St. James and St. Paul's Episcopal

Churches in the city of Richmond—and the Ladies' Aid Society, nearly seventy-five ladies at any given time gathered around Mary Lyon Jones, the Cary girls, and others to stitch flags for the army using Mary's prototype. In all, more than four hundred ladies were enlisted and participated in the project.[34]

There were many notable women in the sewing circles, including Caroline Beauregard, the wife of General Beauregard, who was known to have stitched together the flag that was given to the Eighth Virginia Infantry. Another was Katherine Hill, wife of then Col. A.P. Hill. "Kitty," as she was known, was the sister of then Capt. John Hunt Morgan of Kentucky. Kitty gave her flag, made in part from her bridal clothes, to Hill's Thirteenth Virginia Infantry.[35]

The flags had to be made with haste. The sewing circles worked feverishly, cutting the silk in the prescribed shapes and arrangements of colors. The red fields were made from two double-strips of silk cut from sixteen and one-half inch bolts. Fringe or trim, as long as it was available, was added to some of the flags. As the women would finish the basic flags, Lieutenant Selph would take them to the chemist or artists for the application of the gold stars. He worked as hard overseeing the whole project as the ladies did stitching the flags.[36]

Lieutenant Selph had to make sure the whole endeavor was kept strictly confidential. After all, neither Congress nor the War Department had authorized the design. In spite of Selph's Herculean efforts, the awareness of the design spread throughout Richmond and even to the army at Centreville. "How could General Johnston expect four or five hundred female tongues to be silent on the subject?" recalled a contemporary. "No harm was done by the disclosure, however, and when next the brave troops of the Confederacy went into the fight, those flags were seen dancing in the breeze."[37]

Chapter Five

"Your Mothers, Your Wives and Your Sisters Have Made It"

Once at Centreville, General Johnston placed the divisions of Generals Van Dorn and Longstreet along the ground between Union Mills and the village of Centreville; Van Dorn held the right. Maj. Gen. Gustavus Woodson Smith's division formed the left, "thrown back on the heights nearly parallel to and north of the Warrenton Turnpike. Jackson's division was positioned in the rear of [the village of] Centreville." Engineers were directed to fortify the summit of the hill near the village, and two to three thousand men were directed to occupy them. A series of elaborate forts and earthen defenses connecting the forts were constructed to protect the camps. Those forts and defenses extended east and west of Centreville, all the way across the Leesburg Pike and near to Bull Run on the west and beyond Little Rocky Run to the east. Because of the severe lack of artillery, Johnston's army had to bolster the appearance of the works by using "Quaker guns," imitations of artillery pieces made of logs, and kept near the embrasures in order to present a more fearsome presence to any Federal forces that might approach the defenses.[1]

Behind the defense works, the army began to prepare itself for a long winter encampment. The woodlots in the area were absolutely denuded. The supply of timber in the area was quickly depleted, making it difficult to construct housing for all the troops and supply firewood. More than 1,500 log cabins of various types were built in rows—by company, regiment, and brigade—to house the nearly 32,000 men of Johnston's army. Recalled a soldier in the First Maryland Infantry: "Each company constructed a row

71

of cabins, fronting on a wide street between two companies, the officers' houses at the end of each street and facing down it." Each cabin had a "low door and a small fixed window for which some were lucky enough to procure a pane of glass. Many soldiers got a stove for their cabin; others relied upon a fireplace with a chimney.[2]

Other soldiers built more makeshift quarters. These were small log huts. They were dug into the ground to maximize the shelter from the inclement weather and had log sides and roofs with a wide variety of chimneys. Remembered a captain of the Third South Carolina Infantry:

> Large details were sent out from camp every day to build fortifications for these quarters. This was done by cutting pine poles or logs the right length of our tent, build up three or four feet, and over this pen the tent had to be stretched. They were generally about ten feet square but a man could only stand erect in the middle. The cracks between the logs were chinked with mud, a chimney built out of poles split in half and notched up in the ends of the log parts of the tent. An inside wall was made of plank or small round poles, with space between the walls of five or six inches. This was filled with soft earth or mud, packed tightly, then a blazing fire started, the inner wall burned out, and the dirt baked hard and solid as a brick. In this way we had very good chimneys and comfortable quarters. Forks were driven in the ground on which well placed strong and substantial cross pieces, then round poles, about the size of a man's arm laid over all and thickly strewn with pine needles, on which the blankets were lain.[3]

The rows of log cabins and huts spread out east, south and west of Centreville. Those cabin rows extended west along both sides of the Warrenton Turnpike all the way near Bull Run and onto the Manassas battlefield more than four miles distant; they also extended south all the way to just outside of Manassas Junction, nearly six miles away.[4]

The massive construction of Confederate camps took a toll on the forests in the Centreville area. One resident of the area, Joseph Mills Hanson, claimed "there was enough firewood on our farm to last us for hundreds of years." It quickly vanished. "The southern troops cut down every last bit of it," he wrote.

"They built log houses to live in and they even used our logs to corduroy the road from Centreville to Manassas." The logs were not only used for construction, though. Miller recalled that the Confederates "burned our trees for firewood. We were beginning to worry what we were going to do for wood for ourselves."[5]

Although the main Federal defenses were close to Alexandria, elements of that Federal army slowly advanced closer and closer to Johnston's Centreville defenses. By November, wrote Johnston, the enemy "was nearer to our center than that center to either flank of the army."[6]

The first presentation of flags to regiments of the Confederate Army of the Potomac occurred while the army was constructing winter quarters near Centreville in the fall of 1861; it involved only the commands from Virginia and occurred in early November. Gov. John Letcher had previously announced to General Johnston his intention of supplying blue Virginia State flags to the regiments from the Old Dominion. Private W.H. Morgan of the Eleventh Virginia Infantry remembered that all of the Virginia regiments of his brigade were drawn up around one of the forts constructed for the defenses of the encampment at Centreville. Governor Letcher was in attendance and gave a speech to the troops, all of them lined up in formation. As Letcher presented each flag, the colonel of the regiment walked up to the governor to receive the banner and then gave a brief speech to the men in reply to the governor's words. Morgan remembered that when Col. Eppa Hunton of the Eighth Virginia Infantry received that regiment's flag, he turned to his men, exclaiming: "Every man in Fauquier County shall be carried home feet foremost before their flag will be surrendered!"[7]

Incredibly, Lieutenant Selph was able to complete the construction of the 120 new battle flags for the army by the third week of November 1861; the hundreds upon hundreds of cabins and log huts of Johnston's army were well under construction by then. The sewing circles in Richmond had accomplished an amazing feat; working around the clock, they had procured enough material—and, by shifts, stitched enough flags—to complete the project. It had been a remarkable effort. Mary Henry Lyon Jones and the Cary girls, along with their family and friends from church groups and altar guilds and the Ladies' Aid Society— maybe as many as 400 in all—had done their duty. The flags were brought to army headquarters at Centerville by Lieutenant Selph in late November; it was finally time to present them to the army.[8]

On November 28, 1861 Generals Johnston and Beauregard presented the battle flags the Richmond women had made to the regiments of the Army of the Potomac, including all of those regiments from Virginia. The first regiments to receive the flags were those from General Longstreet's division. Savannah, Georgia, native Col. Moxley Sorrel of General Longstreet's staff recalled that "the day for [the presentation of the flags to] our division went off admirably. It was brilliant weather, and all were in their best outfits, and on their best mounts."[9]

Regiment upon regiment stood in formation in front of Generals Johnston and Beauregard and their staffs. A regimental band played nearby. Behind and around the generals and their staffs a maze of crimson battle flags flapped in the mild breeze. Then Thomas Jordan, the adjutant general of the First Corps, stepped out in front of the dressed ranks. A forty-two-year-old native of Luray, Virginia, Jordan was an 1840 graduate of West Point; one of his roommates there was none other than William T. Sherman. After service in the Seminole and Mexican Wars, he resigned his commission in the army in 1861 and offered his services to the Confederacy. Jordan quickly became Beauregard's adjutant general. So close was he to Beauregard that he, in the words of professor James I. Robertson, Jr., came to regard himself as Beauregard's alter ego. Jordon addressed the thousands of officers and soldiers in front of him, all drawn up in a "hollow square," by reading General Order No. 75, issued "near Centreville" that day by General Beauregard. That order explicitly singled out the women of the city of Richmond who stitched the battle flags together. Jordan's voice was audible throughout the dense ranks:

A new banner is entrusted to-day as a battle flag, to the safe-keeping of the Army of the Potomac.
SOLDIERS: Your mothers, your wives and your sisters have made it. Consecrated by their hands, it must lead you to substantial victory, and the complete triumph of our cause. It can never be surrendered, save to your unspeakable dishonor and with consequences fraught

with immeasurable evil. Under its untarnished folds beat back the invader, and find nationality, everlasting immunity from an atrocious despotism, and honor and renown for yourselves—or death.

By command of General Beauregard.[10]

As the number and state of each regiment was called aloud, its colonel dismounted and walked forward, coming to attention in front of Generals Johnston and Beauregard. After Beauregard made a few remarks, he presented the banner to the colonel. Each colonel responded to Beauregard's remarks so that his regiment could hear them. As each colonel returned to his regiment, his men were ordered to "present." The men snapped to attention and, in unison, brought their muskets to an upright position

HEAD QUARTERS,
1st Corps, Army of the Potomac,
Near Centreville, Nov. 28, 1861.

General Orders
No. 75.

A new banner is entrusted to-day, as a battle-flag, to the safe keeping of the Army of the Potomac.

Soldiers : Your mothers, your wives and your sisters have made it. Consecrated by their hands, it must lead you to substantial victory, and the complete triumph of our cause. It can never be surrendered, save to your unspeakable dishonor and with consequences fraught with immeasurable evil. Under its untarnished folds beat back the invader, and find nationality, everlasting immunity from an atrocious despotism, and honor and renown for yourselves—or death.

By command of General BEAUREGARD.

Thomas Jordan
A. A. Gen'l.

Original imprint of General Order No. 75, dated November 28, 1861, signed by Thomas Jordan, adjutant general of Beauregard's First Corps. This was the order read to the troops when the battle flags were presented on November 28, 1861, and thereafter. (Courtesy of Lewis Leigh, Jr., Leesburg, Virginia) against their chests. The color company was then handed the flag by the colonel to the sound of "deafening cheers."[11]

A soldier in the Fourth South Carolina Infantry remembered the ceremony. "It was," he wrote, "the grandest time we have ever had." Recalling General Beauregard's order never to surrender the flag his regiment was given, he noted: "We will most assuredly obey that order." "The noise the men made was deafening," he continued. "I felt at the time that I could whip a whole brigade of the enemy myself. . . ." Another order from General Beauregard was then read by Adjutant General Jordan to the troops.

> In the event of an action with the enemy, the new battle flag recently issued to the regiments of this army corps will alone be carried on the field. Meantime, regimental commanders will accustom their men to the flag, so that they may be thoroughly acquainted with it.[12]

Pvt. Sam Payne of the Nineteenth Virginia Infantry wrote to his cousin "Mollie" on December 1, 1861, about the impressive ceremony and accompanying orders. He had previously attended the ceremony when Governor Letcher of Virginia had presented the state banners to the regiments from the Old Dominion. That ceremony must have paled in comparison to the presentation by Generals Johnston and Beauregard of the battle flags made by the Richmond women. Payne wrote:

> [The flag we were given] is called a battle flag to be used only in an engagement. I think it much the prettiest one we have. It is beautiful read [sic] silk with a deep blue cross on it and a stare [sic] representing each State in a cross.

The next division to receive flags was General Van Dorn's; his was followed by the divisions of Generals Smith and Jackson.[13]

For regiments of the Confederate Army of the Potomac stationed at advance posts in Fairfax County and in Loudoun County, Virginia, ceremonies presenting new battle flags were held well into December. The regiments in the brigade commanded by Brig. Gen. Daniel Harvey Hill near Leesburg, Virginia, were presented battle flags on December 9, 1861. There Adjutant General Jordan read General Beauregard's orders, and the flags were presented to the four regiments in the same manner as was conducted at Centreville on November 28.[14]

The flags the Richmond ladies made would be carried through the fighting on the Peninsula in June and July 1862, Cedar Mountain and Second Manassas in August, and South Mountain and Sharpsburg in September. Most, by then, would have been in tatters, though some would actually last through the fighting at Fredericksburg in December.[15]

Lieutenant Selph remembered that the Cary girls themselves made three special silk flags in November and December 1861 based on Mary Henry Lyon Jones's prototype. Hetty Cary had the first choice and determined to make hers for Gen. Joseph E. Johnston, the army commander. That certainly fit Hetty; Constance once said to diarist Mary Chesnut: "Hetty likes them that way, you know, gilt-edged and with stars." Jennie Cary chose

Gen. P.G.T. Beauregard. Probably because Constance Cary was a native of Port Gibson, Mississippi, like Maj. Gen. Earl Van Dorn, then one of Johnston's division commanders at Centreville—and because she was last to select—she chose to give the flag she stitched together to General Van Dorn. Van Dorn was also handsome and dashing. Constance claimed she predicted great fame and success for him. "I had never seen Van Dorn," she wrote, "and was rather alarmed at my temerity in selecting him. . . ."[16]

Silk material was delivered to the Cary girls by none other than the brother of Hetty and Jennie, Wilson

Gen. Earl Van Dorn, a carte-de-visite *photograph.* (Courtesy of the Alabama Department of Archives and History, Montgomery, Alabama)

Miles Cary, and Maj. Andrew Dewees Banks, the *vivandiere* of the "Cary Invincibles." Constance noted: "I had to content myself with a poor quality of red silk for the field . . . necessitating an interlining—which I regretted." To the oft-quoted story that she and her sisters used the materials from their own dresses to make the flags, Constance wrote that "[they] possessed no wearing apparel in the flamboyant hues of poppy red and vivid dark blue required." Not being given enough silk, edging, and thread, Constance recalled that she "had a great search for materials." The Cary girls obtained whatever other silk they needed from merchants and wholesalers in Richmond and elsewhere to make their flags. "For materials," Constance remembered, "we ransacked the Richmond shops, but the only red of the shade desired was, to our sorrow, of so thin a textile as to need interlining, hence my flag had to be patched repeatedly [as the war progressed], obscuring some of the stars."[17]

Constance left Richmond to accompany her mother at the hospitals at Culpeper Court House. At Culpeper Court House, she stitched together the silk battle flag for General Van Dorn. When completed, Constance gave the flag to one of Van Dorn's staff officers who frequently visited her at Culpeper Court House. The flag Constance gave Van Dorn actually bears her name, "Constance," which she embroidered in gold thread on an arm of the blue saltire. With the flag was a note from Constance, dated November 10, which read:

> Will General Van Dorn honour me by accepting a flag which I have taken great pleasure in making, and now send with an earnest prayer that the work of my hand may hold its place near him as he goes out to a glorious struggle—and, God willing, may one day wave over the recaptured batteries of my home near the downtrodden Alexandria?
>
> I am, very respectfully, Genl. Van Dorn's obedient servant,
> Constance Cary

Two days later, one of Van Dorn's staff officers found Constance busy stitching clothes and blankets at a hospital at Culpeper Court House. He handed her a small package; it contained a note from Van Dorn. He wrote:

Dear Lady:

The beautiful flag made by your hands and presented to me with the prayer that it should be borne by my side in the impending struggle for the existence of our country, is an appeal to me as a soldier as alluring as the promises of glory; but when you express the hope, in addition, that it may one day wave over the re-captured city of your nativity, your appeal becomes a supplication so beautiful and holy that I were craven-spirited indeed, not to respond to it with all the ability that God has given me. Be assured, dear young lady, that it shall wave over your home if Heaven smiles upon our cause, and I live, and that there shall be written upon it by the side of your name which it now bears, "Victory, Honor and Independence."

In the meantime, I shall hope that you may be as happy as you, who have the soul thus to cheer the soldier on to noble deeds and to victory—should be, and that the flowers want to blossom by your window, may bloom as sweetly for you next May, as they ever did, to welcome you home again.

Very truly and respectfully, dear lady, I am your humble and obedient servant.

Earl Van Dorn
Major General P.A.C.S.[18]

Constance fondly recalled the story that an officer on Van Dorn's staff related to her about the receipt of her flag at the general's headquarters. When it was received and adopted into the division, she was told, a young officer at Van Dorn's headquarters stood up, unsheathed his sword and held it hilt downward upon the table, while one after the other of his comrades clasped the blade, all answering to abide by Constance's prayer that it would one day "wave over the recaptured batteries of [her] home near the downtrodden Alexandria." The officers then drank to the flag and Constance.[19]

Hetty and Jennie Cary actually left Richmond too, but they journeyed to Charlottesville. In that town were many of the Carys' closest relatives. It was to visit all of them that Hetty and Jennie frequently took trips to Charlottesville. There they boarded with their aunt, Mrs. Sydney Carr, the widow of Dabney S. Carr, the brother of the Cary girls' mother. Dabney S. Carr was a newspaper publisher and United States minister at Istanbul, Turkey, from 1843 to 1849. His grandfather—and the Cary girls' great-grandfather—Dabney Carr, is buried in the Jefferson Cemetery at Monticello. Dabney S. Carr died on March 24, 1854. His widow, the former Sydney Smith Nicholas, operated a boarding house at what is now known as Carr's Hill in Charlottesville. Mrs. Carr's ancestor, Wilson Cary Nicholas, is also buried at Monticello. On the site of Carr's Hill now stands the president's home at the University of Virginia. In that boarding house, on Carr's Hill, Hetty and Jennie Cary stitched together the silk battle flags for Generals Johnston and Beauregard.[20]

Both Hetty and Jennie had the gold stars applied to their flags by a chemistry professor at the university. Both flags were sent on December 12, 1861; the couriers taking the flags to the two generals were Wilson Miles Cary and Major Banks. Jennie Cary penned a note from the "University of Virginia" to General Beauregard and enclosed it with her flag. It read:

> I take the liberty of offering the accompanying banner to General Beauregard, soliciting for my handiwork the place of honor upon the battlefield near our renowned and gallant leader. I entrust to him with a fervent prayer that it may wave over victorious plains, and in full confidence that the brilliant success which has crowned his arms throughout or struggle for independence is earnest of future triumphs yet more glorious. In my own home— unhappy Baltimore—a people writhing neath oppression's heel await in agonized expectancy "the triumph-tread of the peerless Beauregard." Will he not, then, bear this banner onward and liberate them from a thralldom worse than death? I am very respectfully Genl. Beauregard's obedient servant.
>
> Jennie Cary

Three days later, Wilson Miles Cary and Major Banks returned to Charlottesville and handed Jennie a note from Beauregard:

> Dear Lady,
>
> I accept with unfeigned pleasure the beautiful Banner (the Battle Flag of the Army of the Potomac) you have been kind enough to make for me, accompanied with the request that it should occupy

Mary Henry Lyon Jones, portrait painted by L.M.D. Guillaume in Richmond, Virginia, in 1859. (Courtesy of Mary Lyon Booth Verlin, Jacksonville, Florida)

The original Southern Cross, the battle flag made by Mary Henry Lyon Jones. (Courtesy of Lon W. Keim, MD, Omaha, Nebraska)

James Alfred Jones, a portrait by an unknown artist. (Courtesy of James Alfred Tyler, Charles City, Virginia)

Bluff Hall, Demopolis, Alabama. The home of Francis Strother Lyon, where Mary Henry Lyon Jones was raised. (Courtesy of the Library of Congress)

Nicola Marschall, a self portrait made about the time he designed the Stars and Bars. (Courtesy of the Alabama Department of Archives and History, Montgomery, Alabama)

The Stars and Bars as it looked when it was approved by the Confederate Congress on March 4, 1861. (Courtesy of the Alabama Department of Archives and History, Montgomery, Alabama)

A secession flag made at the time of the secession of Louisiana, January 26, 1861. (Courtesy of Lon W. Keim, MD, Omaha, Nebraska)

The Battle Flag of the Seventh Georgia Infantry. Col. Francis S. Bartow was grasping this flag when he was mortally wounded during the Battle of Manassas. (Courtesy of the Alabama Department of Archives and History, Montgomery, Alabama)

The battle flag of the Fourth Alabama Infantry. Pointing to this flag during the Battle of Manassas, Gen. Bernard Bee asked what regiment was there. His men responded: "Don't you recognize your own men?" (Courtesy of the Alabama Department of Archives and History, Montgomery, Alabama)

Model of a stained glass window for St. James Episcopal Church in Richmond, Virginia, dedicated to "Captain" Sally Tompkins. Note the likeness of Sally Tompkins, the Robertson Hospital at the top, the wounded being helped off the train at the bottom, and the riband showing all the battles from which wounded were brought to Sally's hospital. (Courtesy of the Library of Congress)

State seal battle flag of the Twenty-Eighth Virginia Infantry, presented in November 1861. This was one of the flags ordered by Gov. John Letcher of Virginia and presented to Virginia regiments at Centreville and other locations in November 1861. (Courtesy of the Museum of the Confederacy, Richmond, Virginia. Photography by Katherine Wetzel)

Lt. Colin McRae Selph meets Mary Henry Lyon Jones. (From the documentary production of *The Southern Cross*)

Mary Henry Lyon Jones and her sewing circle making battle flags. (From the documentary production of *The Southern Cross*)

Flags made by the ladies of Richmond

Flag presented to the headquarters of Maj. Gen. Gustavus Woodson Smith in November 1861. (Courtesy of the Museum of the Confederacy, Richmond, Virginia. Photography by Katherine Wetzel)

Flag presented to the First Virginia Infantry in November 1861. (Courtesy of the Museum of the Confederacy, Richmond, Virginia)

Flag presented to the Eighth Virginia Infantry in November 1861 and made by Caroline Beauregard in Richmond, Virginia. The battle honors were painted on the flag much later. (Courtesy of the Museum of the Confederacy, Richmond, Virginia)

Never-before-published photograph of Hetty Carr Cary, taken in Richmond, Virginia, during the war. From the collection of Judie Flowers. (Courtesy of Blane Piper)

Headquarters flag made by Hetty Cary while in Charlottesville, Virginia, and presented by her to Gen. Joseph E. Johnston in December 1861. (Courtesy of the Museum of the Confederacy, Richmond, Virginia. Photography by Katherine Wetzel)

Never-before-published photograph of Jane Margaret "Jennie" Cary taken in Richmond, Virginia, during the war. From the collection of Judie Flowers. (Courtesy of Blane Piper)

The headquarters flag made by Jennie Cary and presented by her to General Beauregard in December 1861. (Courtesy of the Louisiana State Museum. Gift of the Washington Artillery Battalion)

Flag made by the ladies of Richmond and presented to the Fifteenth Alabama Infantry in November 1861. (Courtesy of the Alabama Department of Archives and History, Montgomery)

The First Battle Flags *by Don Troiani. Troiani's magnificent rendition of the presentation of the first battle flags carefully records what it was like at the Centreville, Virginia, camps on November 28, 1861. Note General Beauregard handing a flag to a regimental commander and the log cabins in the background.* (Painting by Don Troiani)

Hand-painted likeness of Constance Fairfax Cary. (Courtesy of the Virginia Historical Society, Richmond, Virginia)

Detail of the headquarters flag made by Constance Fairfax Cary and presented to General Van Dorn, showing the name "Constance" embroidered on an arm of the cross by Miss Cary. (Courtesy of the Museum of the Confederacy, Richmond, Virginia. Photography by Katherine Wetzel)

Headquarters flag made by Constance Fairfax Cary and presented by her to Gen. Earl Van Dorn in late November 1861. (Courtesy of the Museum of the Confederacy, Richmond, Virginia. Photography by Katherine Wetzel)

The Hardee-pattern battle flag of the Twenty-Fourth Mississippi Infantry carried through the battles of Shiloh and Perryville. (Courtesy of the Museum of the Confederacy, Richmond, Virginia. Photography by Katherine Wetzel)

The Stars and Bars battle flag of the Sixth Kentucky Infantry carried through the battle of Shiloh. (Courtesy of the Museum of the Confederacy, Richmond, Virginia. Photography by Katherine Wetzel)

The Fifth Company of the Washington Artillery of New Orleans opens fire with Mary Henry Lyon Jones's battle flag flying nearby. (From the documentary production of *The Southern Cross*)

The Polk-pattern battle flag of the Sixteenth Tennessee Infantry carried through the battles of Shiloh and Perryville. (Courtesy of the Museum of the Confederacy, Richmond, Virginia. Photography by Katherine Wetzel)

The fighting in the Hornet's Nest, Shiloh, April 6, 1862. (Courtesy of the Library of Congress)

One of the panels from the panorama of The Army of the Cumberland *painted by William Travis. Note the Bottom House on the left, General Adams' Confederate brigade at the fence, the Federal Fifteenth Kentucky Infantry on the ridge, and the Bottom barn on fire from the exploding shells of the Fifth Company.* (Courtesy of the Armed Forces History Division, National Museum of American History, Smithsonian Institution)

Confederate column attacks through the dense woods at the battle of Chickamauga, where Lieutenant Blair was killed on September 19, 1863. (Courtesy of the Library of Congress)

Headstone at the grave of Lt. Thomas Blair, Fifth Company, Washington Artillery of New Orleans, at the Spring Hill Cemetery, Mobile, Alabama. Blair was killed at Chickamauga, September 19, 1863. (Courtesy of H. Pell Brown, Jr., Mobile, Alabama)

Capt. Cuthbert H. Slocumb prepares to hand Mary Henry Lyon Jones's battle flag to Lt. Thomas Blair. (From the documentary production of *The Southern Cross*)

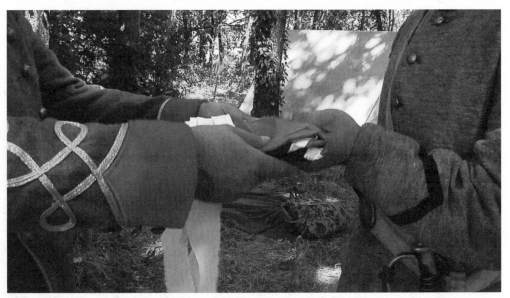

Captain Slocumb hands Mary Henry Lyon Jones's battle flag to Lieutenant Blair. (From the documentary production of *The Southern Cross*)

Mary Henry Lyon Jones. The portrait was probably painted in Richmond, Virginia, not long before she died. (Courtesy of Mary Lyon Booth Verlin, Jacksonville, Florida)

Headstone near the graves of Mary Henry Lyon Jones and James Alfred Jones in the Hollywood Cemetery, Richmond, Virginia. (Courtesy of Lon W. Keim, MD, Omaha, Nebraska)

Close-up of the inscription on the headstone of Mary Henry Lyon Jones and James Alfred Jones in Hollywood Cemetery, Richmond, Virginia. (Courtesy of Lon W. Keim, MD, Omaha, Nebraska)

University of Virginia
December 12th/61

I take the liberty of offering the accompanying banner to Genl Beauregard, soliciting for my handiwork the place of honor upon the battle-field near our renowned and gallant leader—

I entrust it to him with a fervent prayer that it may wave over victorious plains, and in full confidence that the brilliant success which has crowned his arms throughout our struggle for independence is an earnest of future

triumphs yet more glorious. In my own home unhappy Baltimore— a people writhing neath oppression's heel await in agonized expectancy "the triumph-tread of the peerless Beauregard"— Will he not, then, bear this banner onward and liberate them from a thralldom worse than death?

I am very respectfully
Genl Beauregard's
obedient servant
Jennie Cary.

The original letter written to General Beauregard by Jennie Cary while in Charlottesville, Virginia, on December 12, 1861. With the letter, Jennie Cary sent the headquarters flag she made for Beauregard. (Courtesy of Lewis Leigh, Jr., Leesburg, Virginia)

near me the place of honor on the battlefield. It shall be borne by my personal escort; and protected by a just Providence, the sanctity of our Cause, and the valor of our troops, it will lead us on from victory to victory until you shall have the proud satisfaction of waving it with your own fair hands as a signal of triumph, from the top of the Washington Monument in your own native city— Baltimore. With high respect and consideration, I remain, Dear Lady, your most obedient and devoted servant.

G. T. Beauregard, General Commanding

That flag was kept by General Beauregard throughout the war and was draped over his casket when he died.[21]

All the Cary flags had common attributes: the saltires were made of dark blue silk and the fields were made of a double layer of thin scarlet silk. The five-pointed stars—twelve in all—of Hetty

The original field copy of the letter General Beauregard wrote to Jennie Cary on December 15, 1861, thanking her for the headquarters flag she made for him. (Courtesy of Lewis Leigh, Jr., Leesburg, Virginia) and Jennie Cary's flags were painted on the flags by a chemistry professor at the University of Virginia. The flag made by Constance Cary had twelve five-pointed stars that were painted on the saltire by "a professional flag maker in Richmond," Constance recalled. She said she "lacked the material (and perhaps the skill) to add them appropriately." All of the Cary flags had gold metallic fringe; all of them were made using Mary Henry Lyon Jones's prototype. From Mary Henry Lyon Jones's first Southern Cross, the St. Andrew's Cross battle flag became the single most recognizable emblem of the Confederacy.[22]

Chapter Six

"Gayety Was the Most Marked Feature about Them"

And what happened to the flag made by Mary Henry Lyon Jones? Well, it was given to none other than Maj. James Burdge Walton, commander of the Washington Artillery Battalion of New Orleans. He could have kept it, but that was not to be.[1]

With the fall of Forts Henry and Donelson along the Tennessee and Kentucky border in February 1862, Gen. Albert Sidney Johnston, the commander of the western Department Number Two, issued a call for more troops. A native of Washington, Kentucky, Johnston was an 1826 graduate of West Point. He served in the Black Hawk War and then went to Texas, where he became chief commander of the army of the Republic of Texas. He had also served as secretary of war for the Republic of Texas from 1838 to 1840. As a commander of Texas volunteers, Johnston served in the Mexican War. Reappointed to the United States Army in 1849, he became the colonel of the Second United States Cavalry. His lieutenant colonel was none other than Robert E. Lee. Johnston led the Utah expedition against the Mormons in 1857 and commanded the Department of Utah. He resigned his commission in May 1861 and was appointed full general in the Confederate army in August 1861. Johnston was charged to defend all of the territory from the Appalachian Mountains to the Mississippi River and beyond. After the fall of Forts Henry and Donelson, Johnston's thin Confederate ranks had retreated out of Kentucky and were on the brink of giving up Tennessee.[2]

Responding to General Johnston's call was the Fifth Company of the Washington Artillery of New Orleans. The company was commanded by twenty-eight-year-old Capt. Washington Irving Hodgson, a native of Louisville, Kentucky. After moving to New Orleans at age fourteen, he served as a clerk with a hardware company before joining the auction house of James Burdge Walton in 1851. Although first attached to the Fourth Company of the Washington Artillery as a lieutenant, Hodgson remained in New Orleans to organize a reserve corps (which evolved into the Fifth Company) after the original four companies—under the command of Major Walton—were transferred to Richmond, Virginia in May 1861. Hodgson was elected captain of the Fifth Company in June 1861.[3]

Joining the Fifth Company in March 1862 was Cuthbert Harrison Slocumb, a thirty-one-year-old native of New Orleans. The son of Samuel B. and Cora A. Slocumb, he was a hardware merchant and senior partner in Slocumb, Baldwin & Company in New Orleans before the war. He and his family had amassed considerable wealth. Slocumb was married to the former Abby Hannah Day; the couple entertained lavishly before the war in

Members of the Fifth Company of the Washington Artillery of New Orleans camp near New Orleans. Miller, Photographic History of the Civil War, *I:199.* (Courtesy of the Library of Congress)

their enormous brick residence next to the municipal building in New Orleans. Slocumb enlisted in the Washington Artillery in May 1861 and became assistant quartermaster; he was elevated to the rank of first lieutenant in the Second Company and accompanied it to Richmond, Virginia, that month. Slocumb distinguished himself at the First Battle of Manassas, winning praise from Major Walton. Slocumb's twelve-pound howitzers supported Brigadier General Ewell's brigade at Union Mills not far from General Beauregard's headquarters. Slocumb abruptly resigned from the Second Company in November 1861 but re-enlisted in the Fifth Company on March 6, 1862. A first lieutenant, Slocumb became section commander.[4]

Other lieutenants and section commanders in the Fifth Company were Tennessee-born William Crumm Darrah Vaught, also known as "Billie," a clerk in New Orleans when the war began, and the Creole Joseph Adolpho "Jack" Chalaron, a thirty-six-year-old New Orleans native and graduate of Louisiana College. He had been a clerk in a merchandizing business in New Orleans before entering the army. Parenthetically, Chalaron would later prove to be instrumental in collecting information about Mary Henry Lyon Jones's flag. He would first solicit Colin McRae Selph to write his memoirs of securing the first St. Andrew's Cross battle flag for the army. Chalaron would perform those tasks after the war as an officer of the Washington Artillery of New Orleans camp of the United Confederate Veterans and their Memorial Hall in New Orleans. There was also Lt. Edson L. Hews, a twenty-three-year-old native of the Crescent City who had been a clothing salesman before the war.[5]

The officers and men of the Fifth Company were trained in what is now Audubon Park in New Orleans. The men called the training site "Camp Lewis;" it was located near a village then called Carrollton, "several miles from the city." The battery consisted of 156 men and six bronze guns: two model 1841 six-pound smooth bores, two six-pound rifled guns, and two twelve-pound howitzers. For months, the cannoneers had posed and clowned for photographers. The company was, for a time, the toast of the Crescent City. The Fifth Company boasted men from New Orleans, as well as every state in the South, and Kentucky,

Cuthbert H. Slocumb, from a carte-de-visite *photograph.* (Courtesy of the late William A. Turner, La Plata, Maryland)

Joseph Adolpho "Jack" Chalaron, from a carte-de-visite *photograph.* (Courtesy of the late William A. Turner, La Plata, Maryland)

Illinois, New England, New York, Germany, Ireland, England, Scotland, France, and Canada, illustrating the cosmopolitan nature of the city of New Orleans. It was to the Fifth Company of the Washington Artillery of New Orleans that Maj. James Burdge Walton gave the battle flag made by Mary Henry Lyon Jones—the first "Southern Cross."[6]

The Fifth Company was prepared to move north to join Gen. Albert Sidney Johnston's army at Corinth, Mississippi. The battery was sworn into Confederate service in Lafayette Park in New Orleans. After a service at the First Presbyterian Church, the Fifth Company assembled at Jackson Depot and boarded the train along with the Crescent Regiment of New Orleans, the Twenty-Fourth Louisiana Infantry.[7]

At Corinth, on March 31, 1862, it became part of Gen. Braxton Bragg's Corps of Johnston's Confederate Army of the Mississippi. Bragg, the corps commander, was a native of Warrenton, North Carolina, and an 1837 graduate of West Point. He fought the Seminoles and served through the Mexican War with great gallantry. Resigning from the army in 1856, Bragg became a planter in Louisiana, managing plantations owned by his wife's family. He was appointed brigadier general in the Confederate army in March 1861 and was assigned to command all of the newly-raised troops who were trained at posts along the coast—from Pensacola, Florida, to Mobile. It was from Mobile that Bragg responded to General Johnston's call for reinforcements. He rapidly moved his forces north on the Mobile and Ohio Railroad to join Johnston's army at Corinth.[8]

The Rev. P.D. Stevenson, who then was serving in an Arkansas regiment, recalled being at Corinth just before the battle of Shiloh. He had "strayed to the [railroad] depot [where he] found a scene of great activity, of the constant coming of new commands, of the greeting of old acquaintances belonging to the different troops, and meeting now for the first time since enlistment." He recalled the Fifth Company in bivouac "not far from the depot" and the Tishomingo Hotel that stood next to where the Memphis and Charleston Railroad tracks crossed those of the Mobile and Ohio Railroad. "They had just quit the cars," Stevenson wrote, "their uniforms were fresh; their spirits high; they sang and joked

and laughed aloud as they cooked their meals at the camp fire."
Stevenson continued: "Gayety was the most marked feature
about them. It attracted general attention. I found afterwards
that that feature marked that battery permanently all through
the checkered experiences of its subsequent splendid career."[9]

The Fifth Company's silk St. Andrew's Cross battle flag was an
oddity in Johnston's army. Only General Beauregard, then newly-
named second-in-command to General Johnston, flew anything
like it; Beauregard's headquarters flag was the one made for him
by Jennie Cary. In Johnston's army were odd Latin cross Polk
flags, silver moon Hardee flags, state banners, and, of course, a
profusion of Stars and Bars. The Polk flags resembled the
rectangular sovereignty flags that were popular during the
secession of the slave states. The only difference was that the

*The Tishomingo Hotel, Corinth, Mississippi. Alongside the hotel the
Fifth Company set up its first camp with the Army of the Mississippi
before the battle of Shiloh. Miller,* Photographic History of the Civil War,
II:138-139. (Courtesy of the Library of Congress)

field of the Polk flag was blue, not red, and the cross was red, not blue. The Hardee flags were unlike anything else. They consisted of nothing more than a blue field edged in white with a large white full moon or oval in the center.[10]

The Fifth Company moved out of Corinth with the rest of Johnston's army on April 3 and marched through heavy rains until April 5. The army was being led to attack Gen. Ulysses S. Grant's Army of the Tennessee. In March, Grant's forces had ascended the Tennessee River from Paducah, Kentucky, all the way to Pittsburg Landing, about twenty miles north of Corinth. Since then, Grant's five divisions had set up camps throughout the area between Owl and Lick Creeks and south all the way past the log Shiloh Methodist Church. There a veritable sea of tents, wagon parks, hospitals, sutler tents, and quartermaster and subsistence depots had been established. Between Pittsburg Landing and Shiloh Methodist Church was a veritable armed city, complete with steamboats coming to and going from the landing, bringing troops and supplies. Massive timber-clad gunboats patrolled the river, protecting the camps. With an army of more than 50,000 officers and men, Grant's encampments presented a breathtaking spectacle in those clearings formerly inhabited only by small subsistence and cotton farm families.[11]

Then, on April 6, the Fifth Company, carrying the silk battle flag wrought from the hands of Mary Henry Lyon Jones, fought its way up the Corinth-Pittsburg Landing Road with Bragg's corps to the Shiloh Methodist Church, blasting Gen. William T. Sherman's surprised regiments in one camp after another. The "two howitzers and two rifled guns under the command of Lieutenants Slocumb and Vaught," assisted by two more guns from a neighboring battery, "soon silenced [the enemy's] guns and had the extreme gratification of seeing our brave and gallant troops charge through [the enemy] camps, running the enemy before them at the point of the bayonette," wrote the Fifth Company's commander. Sherman's division collapsed; its men fleeing in the face of the Confederate onslaught. By 2:00 p.m., the Fifth Company was unlimbering to open fire on the sixth enemy camp.[12]

The Federal forces withdrew until rallied by Gens. Benjamin F. Prentice and W.H.L. Wallace in the woods and dense brush along a sunken farm lane. There, in what would become known as "the Hornet's Nest," the broken Federal forces made a last stand.[13]

Tragedy struck as General Johnston was mortally wounded, possibly the result of friendly fire. Beauregard took over command.[14]

Along much of the line, Confederate infantry attacked the Hornet's Nest multiple times. It was an indescribably bloody affair. Kentucky-born Col. Randall Lee Gibson of Terrebonne Parish, Louisiana, led his brigade of Louisiana and Arkansas troops against the Hornet's Nest four distinct times; his losses were staggering. The commander of Gibson's own Thirteenth Louisiana Infantry, Maj. A.P. Anegno, was mortally wounded, as was the captain who took Anegno's place as regimental commander. Col. William H. Stephens's brigade pressed ahead toward the Federal positions in the dense thickets alongside Gibson's brigade; it too was decimated.[15]

Around 3 o'clock in the afternoon, Brig. Gen. Daniel Ruggles, a hard-nosed 1833 graduate of West Point and a veteran of the Mexican War, collected the better part of eleven Confederate batteries. General Beauregard actually brought forward elements of the Fifth Company; others were brought forward by staff officers of General Ruggles. They unleashed a withering fire primarily into the regiments of General W.H.L. Wallace's division in the Hornet's Nest until late in the afternoon. Federal General Wallace was mortally wounded. Finally, the Federal forces in the Hornet's Nest were surrendered by General Prentiss.[16]

The Fifth Company had fought well. However, its commander, Captain Hodgson, had been "indisposed" in the rear. Much of the action was performed under the command of Lt. Cuthbert Slocumb, who had performed well. Lt. William Crumm Darrah Vaught and Lt. Joseph Adolpho "Jack" Chalaron had also served admirably.

The Fifth Company was pulled back to a position not far from the log Shiloh Methodist Church, which had been turned into a hospital. There the men counted their losses; three cannoneers had been killed and eight wounded on April 6. The cannoneers were parched with thirst. Lieutenant Chalaron recalled finding some water in Shiloh Creek below the church where the battery first engaged the enemy that morning. The men drank the water out of the creek only to find out the next morning that the "lopped off limbs of our wounded" had been thrown into the creek bed. Many had commented that night on the "peculiar and sweet taste of the water," little suspecting the cause until morning.[17]

April 7 was to prove heart-wrenching; Gen. Ulysses S. Grant's broken Federal Army of the Tennessee, reinforced by the arrival of Gen. Don Carlos Buell's Army of the Ohio during the night, counterattacked. Buell, a native of Ohio, grew up in Lawrenceburg, Indiana, and graduated from West Point in 1841. A veteran of the Mexican War and service along the Pacific coast, Buell was appointed a brigadier general in May 1861. Gen. George B. McClellan placed him in command of the Federal army, named the Army of the Ohio, that seized Kentucky and then entered Tennessee upon the fall of Fort Donelson in February 1862. He was summoned to move his army from Columbia to Savannah, Tennessee, to reinforce Grant's army well before the fighting erupted at Shiloh.[18]

In spite of furious resistance, the combined Federal armies pressed ahead on the early morning hours of April 7. Still without a captain, the Fifth Company was led by Lieutenant Slocumb. The Confederate lines began to give way; refugees from the front lines fled toward the rear, streaming across the open fields, abandoned Federal camps and thick woods, and through the bivouac site of the Fifth Company.

Along with the Nineteenth Louisiana Infantry and the Crescent Regiment of New Orleans, the Fifth Company was ordered forward to the "extreme right" of the army by Col. Benjamin L. Hodge. The little command formed a battle line along the Hamburg-Purdy Road; the Crescent Regiment was held in reserve. The Twenty-First Tennessee Infantry fought along the left of the Fifth Company's guns. Maj. Gen. John C. Breckinridge's reserve division had "pushed the enemy" to within several hundred yards of the guns of the Fifth Company. Under the direction of Gen. Hardee, the Fifth Company's six guns blasted the Federal positions ahead of them. In turn, Capt. John Mendenhall's Fourth United States Artillery and Capt. William R. Terrill's Battery H, Fifth United States Artillery, from the Army of the Ohio, returned the fire.[19]

Recalled the orderly sergeant, A. Gordon Bakewell:

Then commenced a terrible artillery duel. In the right of contending armies, and enveloped in the confusion of battle...we became separated from the other section of our command, and were soon left in a forlorn condition, with but five or six of our men unhurt, some horses killed, and others broken loose. Nevertheless, we worked the pieces until they were disabled, so entangled in the underbrush and trees, and so buried in the soft soil, by the recoil, that, with our reduced strength, we could not extricate them.

Bakewell looked ahead of the guns. "I saw a line of Federals about to charge; while in our rear, on turning round, I beheld the New Orleans Crescent regiment coming up in a counter charge, at double-quick," he remembered. "Many on both sides firing as they advanced." He realized it was "worse than useless" to remain between the two contending lines and thus called to the men: "We can do nothing more, let's get out of this or we are all dead men."[20]

Lieutenant Slocumb and Sergeant Benjamin H. Green, along with several enlisted men, were wounded. The company left on the field three of its guns, but not until after it had fired more than 130 rounds into the enemy. As the fighting ended on April 7, the Fifth Company counted its losses: eight killed and twenty-four wounded. Thirty-nine horses were dead or wounded. The battery had expended 723 rounds of ammunition during the two days of fighting. Mary Henry Lyon Jones's battle flag, though, remained in the grasp of the cannoneers. The Confederate army retreated back to Corinth.[21]

Chapter Seven

"[I] Recommend That They . . . Have 'Perryville' Inscribed on Their Banner"

The beaten Confederates retreated further from Corinth, Mississippi to Tupelo. Grant's and Buell's Federal armies seized Corinth. The new commander of the Army of the Mississippi, Gen. Braxton Bragg, was determined to reenter Tennessee and, hopefully, Kentucky in the summer of 1862. To do that, he sent all his infantry by way of the Mobile and Ohio Railroad to Mobile, Alabama, to Atlanta, and then by the Western and Atlantic Railroad, to Chattanooga in August 1862. Bragg's cavalry, baggage trains, and artillery, including the Fifth Company, moved across Alabama to Chattanooga. General Buell's Federal Army of the Ohio raced from Corinth to Nashville. In September, Bragg's Army of the Mississippi skirted Nashville and then entered Kentucky. They were followed by Buell's army, which held Nashville until Bragg entered Kentucky. Then Buell's army methodically followed Bragg's army into the Bluegrass State.[1]

Re-equipped, the Fifth Company consisted of two twelve-pound howitzers, two six-pound smoothbores, and two three-inch rifled guns. It was now commanded by newly-commissioned Capt. Cuthbert H. Slocumb, who had served so well at Shiloh. The battery was assigned to the brigade of Louisiana regiments and battalions commanded by Brig. Gen. Daniel Weisiger Adams; all of the regiments and battalions of Adams' brigade had been bloodied attacking the Hornet's Nest at Shiloh. Adams was a native of Frankfort, Kentucky, who had practiced law in Mississippi and Louisiana before the war. At the outbreak of the war he was the lieutenant colonel of the First Louisiana Regulars. He was later promoted colonel of the regiment. He became a brigade commander on the battlefield at Shiloh after Brig. Gen. Adley Gladden was mortally wounded early in the fighting on April 6. Promoted to brigadier general in May 1862, Adams was assigned to command a brigade of his own.[2]

Adams' brigade consisted of the Sixteenth Louisiana Infantry, Twentieth Louisiana Infantry, Twenty-Fifth Louisiana Infantry, Fourteenth Battalion of Louisiana Sharpshooters, and the Thirteenth Louisiana Infantry. The Thirteenth Louisiana was commanded by Col. Randall Lee Gibson, who had commanded a brigade of Louisiana and Arkansas regiments at Shiloh that was utterly decimated attacking the Hornet's Nest.[3]

Adams' brigade was part of Gen. J. Patton Anderson's division of Gen. William J. Hardee's wing. Hardee, a native of Camden County, Georgia, was an 1838 graduate of West Point and a veteran of the Mexican War. Just before the war, he served as commandant of the cadets at West Point; there he wrote the standard textbook *Rifle and Light Infantry Tactics*, published in 1861. When Georgia seceded from the Union, Hardee resigned his lieutenant colonelship and was appointed a brigadier general in the Confederate army. He served in Arkansas early in the war and had been summoned to join Gen. Albert Sidney Johnston just before the Battle of Shiloh, where he commanded a corps.[4]

On October 1, 1862, General Buell's Federal Army of the Ohio, 54,000 strong, moved out of Louisville against Bragg's army, then at Bardstown and less than half the size of Buell's army. Kentucky was in the midst of a three-month drought; water was scarce. Most of the ponds, creeks, and rivers in the area where Bragg's army campaigned had become bone dry. The crops in central Kentucky had been parched, and food and forage for the horses and mules was hard to find.[5]

Bragg left the army and arrived at Lexington—where he and Maj. Gen. Edmund Kirby Smith, whose Provisional Army of Kentucky had entered the state and defeated a Federal force at Richmond, Kentucky, on August 30—rode to Frankfort, the capital city, to swear in a governor of Confederate Kentucky on October 4. Bragg left Maj. Gen. Leonidas Polk in command of the army at Bardstown. General Polk withdrew the army from

Bardstown in the face of the Federal advance; the withdrawal took the Fifth Company through Springfield and then over the Springfield Pike to the outskirts of Perryville, Kentucky. There a rear guard engagement broke out on October 7 and subsided with nightfall.[6]

Having returned to the army the previous evening, Bragg determined to strike Buell's army just west of Perryville on October 8 in what would be the second and last battle through which Mary Henry Lyon Jones's battle flag would serve. Bragg believed an isolated element of the Federal army was in front of him. He moved Maj. Gen. Benjamin F. Cheatham's division of Polk's wing down the Chaplain River to a location believed to be on the far left Union flank. Cheatham, a hard-fighting, hard-drinking man from Nashville, was forty-two years old. Appointed brigadier general in July 1861 and major general in March 1862, he fought gallantly at Shiloh. In the Kentucky campaign he led fifteen regiments, all but one of which were from Tennessee. The lone regiment not from the Volunteer State was the Forty-First Georgia. Cheatham's three brigades were ably led by Brig. Gens. Daniel S. Donelson, A.P. Stewart, and George P. Maney, all Tennesseeans. They commanded some of the most noted and hard-fighting regiments of the Volunteer State.[7]

General Hardee's wing spread out for over a mile along high ground between Cheatham's left flank and an area just south of Mackville Road. Hardee's regiments flew the odd silver moon Hardee battle flag. With Mary Henry Lyon Jones's battle flag held aloft, the Fifth Company, known now as "Slocumb's Battery," unlimbered and moved into position on a ridge south of Mackville Road, supporting Adams' brigade. In front of Hardee's wing ran Doctor's Fork of the Chaplain River, almost dry due to the three-month draught.[8]

Across the fields, on high ground less than a quarter of a mile away, was the enemy: Brig. Gen. Lovell H. Rousseau's division of Maj. Gen. Alexander McDowell McCook's First Corps. Rousseau was no professional soldier; in fact, he was born not more than twenty miles from where the battle was being fought. With little formal education, he studied law and moved to Bloomfield, Indiana, where he was admitted to the bar. He was elected to the

Indiana State Legislature and served gallantly in the Mexican War as a captain of an Indiana regiment. Returning to Kentucky, he practiced law in Louisville and was elected to the Kentucky State Senate in 1860. He raised the Third Kentucky (Federal) Infantry and was commissioned a colonel. Promoted to brigadier general on October 1, 1861, he ably commanded a brigade at Shiloh. At Perryville, his command was designated the Third Division of McCook's First Army Corps.[9]

A furious cannonade erupted from both sides in the late morning. Then, at 2 o'clock, Cheatham's Confederate division—all of its regiments flying Polk flags—slammed into the Federal left flank, made up of a brigade from the division commanded by Kentucky-born Brig. Gen. James S. Jackson. That Federal brigade was commanded by Virginia-born and West Point-trained Brig. Gen. William Rufus Terrill, who commanded Battery H, Fifth United States Artillery at Shiloh, the very battery that so severely shelled the Fifth Company on April 7. Terrill's regiments were from Ohio and Illinois; some detachments were from East Tennessee and Kentucky. Few of Terrill's infantrymen at Perryville had ever been in combat. General Jackson was mortally wounded while mounted in the midst of Lt. Charles Parsons' eight-gun Improvised Battery of the Fourth United States Artillery, which was spread out along an open knoll in the midst of Terrill's infantry commands. The battery was overrun and all but one of its guns were damaged or captured.[10]

Terrill's raw troops gave way and withdrew to a second ridge where the young brigadier rallied his men alongside a brigade commanded by Wisconsin-born Brig. Gen. John C. Starkweather, a veteran of the First Battle of Manassas from the division of General Rousseau. Major General Cheatham's attack continued through a parched cornfield until it crashed into Starkweather's Wisconsin, Illinois, and Pennsylvania regiments and two Federal artillery batteries from Indiana and Kentucky. Recalled Sam Watkins of the First Tennessee Infantry in Brigadier General Maney's brigade, "We did not recoil, but our line was fairly hurled back by the leaden hail that was poured into our very faces. Eight color bearers were killed at one discharge of their cannon."[11]

There, General Terrill was killed as shrapnel from a bursting shell tore away his left lung. He fell off his horse and plunged to the ground, dead. "It was a life to life and death to death grapple," remembered Watkins. Terrill's last line withdrew to yet a third ridge.[12]

On Cheatham's left, Brigadier Generals Donelson and Stewart struggled against elements of three Federal brigades brought onto the field by General Rousseau. Thomas Head of the Sixteenth Tennessee Infantry in Donelson's brigade remembered that the ranks of his regiment were "mowed down at a fearful rate." They "closed up," he recalled, and continued as "heavy charges of grape and canister were hurled into their ranks from the front and on the flanks." They pressed the assault, and the Federal lines only "yielded [their position] about sundown."[13]

As Cheatham's division struggled through the heavy gunfire, Confederate brigades from Hardee's wing successively moved forward, forcing the Federal lines back upon their supports. First came Col. Thomas M. Jones's Mississippians, just to the left of Cheatham's left wing brigades of Gens. Donelson and Stewart. Jones's men were shredded as General Rousseau brought onto the field fresh infantry and artillery batteries to meet each Confederate assault. Then came Brig. Gen. John C. Brown's brigade of Mississippians and Floridians, followed by Brig. Gen. Sterling A.M. Wood's brigade of Mississippians and Alabamians. Steadily, the Federal division of General Rousseau gave ground until the center of his line had fallen back onto the broken left flank of the Federal army behind a stone fence along Benton Road. The hard-charging Confederates pushed ahead. "We got to within 30 yards of the fence, but our ranks were so badly thinned that we could not get to them," remembered a soldier in the Thirty-Third Alabama Infantry in General Wood's brigade.[14]

To the right of Adams' brigade and the Fifth Company, Brig. Gen. Bushrod R. Johnson's brigade of Tenneseeans, followed by Brig. Gen. Patrick R. Cleburne's Tennesseeans and Arkansans, holding their Hardee flags aloft, stepped out on their way to and across Doctor's Fork and up the steep ridge toward the Federal lines. "We advanced down the open ground into the creek bottom exposed to a heavy fire of artillery and small arms," remembered one of Cleburne's captains. "I ordered the brigade to advance in double-time and we were soon in the rocky bed of the creek so immediately under the enemy that their fire passed harmlessly over us." Cleburne's horse, Dixie, was killed as he crossed the dry, rocky bed of Doctor's Fork.[15]

Adams waited for Col. Samuel Powell's Arkansas brigade to get in line. Powell, however, was delayed and the hour was getting late. Brigadier General Adams proceeded to put his Louisianans in motion toward Doctor's Fork. Through a hail of gunfire from the Federal Fifteenth Kentucky and the Third Ohio Infantry regiments of Col. William Lytle's brigade on the crest of a ridge— alongside six ten-pound Parrott rifles of Battery A of the First Michigan Artillery, commanded by Captain Cyrus O. Loomis— Adams' men swarmed through the farmyard behind the bullet-riddled and shell-pocked Squire Henry P. Bottom House and then drove up the long, steep ridge against the Federal right flank.[16]

The Fifth Company limbered up, moved forward, crossed Doctor's Fork, and unlimbered behind the Bottom House. Mary

Never-before-published photograph of the Squire H.P. Bottom House on the Perryville Battlefield. The Fifth Company unlimbered and went into action behind this house. Note the bullet and shell marks on the west face of the house. (Courtesy of Kent Masterson Brown)

Henry Lyon Jones's battle flag flapped in the sulphurous air alongside the cannoneers. There, the Fifth Company shelled the Federal lines ahead of them. Bursting shells from the Fifth Company set fire to the Bottom barn, which stood on the ridge in the midst of the Kentucky regiment. Black smoke billowed forth, blinding many of those who contested the blood-soaked Bottom fields. The three Confederate brigades continued their assault, pushing the Federal right flank back; the Fifth Company limbered up again and followed the attack force. Cleburne was wounded near the burning Bottom barn. The Federal troops fled in "great disorder, panic and confusion, throwing away their arms and equipments," wrote Brigadier General Adams. Finally, the Federal right flank was driven back nearly a mile by the force of Adams', Cleburne's and Johnson's brigades.[17]

The Federal troops rallied along Benton Road not far from the broken lines of the Federal left. With his hat on the tip of his sword, Brigadier General Rousseau yelled for his men to hold at all costs. The Fifth Company, behind Adams' infantry columns, unlimbered again to blast the Federal lines. Only when Federal artillery from Maj. Gen. Charles Gilbert's Federal corps was brought to bear on the left flank of Adams' brigade and the Fifth Company did General Hardee direct the commands to withdraw. It was 7:30 at night.[18]

Moving back to a position on the ridge east of Doctor's Fork, close to where the battle began, the Fifth Company unlimbered for the last time at Perryville and opened fire. "The shades of night have fallen, and for an hour the guns on each side [fired] at each other's flashes." The enemy finally ceased firing. The Fifth Company, however, was not done. Its cannoneers stood alongside their guns. The barrels were so hot from the constant firing that many of the men's hands had been blistered by them. The Fifth Company then fired the last artillery shot heard along the rolling hills outside of Perryville.[19]

The ammunition chests of the limbers and caissons of the Fifth Company were "mostly empty." The battery had fired 758 rounds since the opening of the battle at 1:00 p.m.[20]

The cannoneers were exhausted. Wrote Lieutenant Chalaron of the Fifth Company: "The fray had been incessant, and our advance continued. Tired from the heat, excitement and hard work, the men had suffered intensely from thirst." Only "the black powder-polluted water of the guns' sponge buckets" gave their thirst any relief. Rumbling down a long ridge behind the last position held by the battery, the men came upon a pool of water, probably near the two-story wooden-frame house owned by John and Elizabeth Bottom Dye, a dwelling that was being used as the field hospital for Maj. Gen. Simon B. Buckner's division. "Our men rushed for it like the others," recalled Chalaron, and, "flat on their bellies, lapped up the water, regardless of the horses that stood in it, and of the bodies of several dead enemies who had been killed in the pool or had dragged themselves there to die." He continued:

> The harvest moon in all its splendor illuminated this gruesome spectacle that but few had noticed in their eagerness to drink, and only became aware of as they arose, their thirst once satisfied. Some stomachs were turned, but most of the company had stomach and sensibilities already steeled by their war experiences.

It was just as it had been at Shiloh.[21]

Perryville had been a ferocious engagement. Nearly ten thousand men fell in less than six hours. Captain Slocumb's cannoneers distinguished themselves; in all, two officers and sixteen men had been wounded. Brigadier General Adams praised the Fifth Company; it "did most essential and valuable service and deserves particular notice of praise," he wrote four days after the battle, "and I would especially recommend that they be allowed to have 'Perryville' inscribed on their banner."[22]

General Bragg withdrew from Perryville that night, retreating to Harrodsburg. On October 12, the army began its withdrawal from Bryantsville, Kentucky, to Cumberland Gap, Tennessee. As Bragg's army came to rest at Murfreesboro, the Fifth Company determined to retire its worn and torn battle flag. A new silver moon Hardee flag was presented to Captain Slocumb and his men.[23]

Slocumb turned to Lt. Thomas Blair, who had been captured at Perryville but exchanged, and who had been given a leave of absence. Slocumb asked him to take Mary Henry Lyon Jones's battle flag to his home at Spring Hill near Mobile, Alabama, for safe keeping. Blair agreed.[24]

Near Mobile, the same city where Mary Henry Lyon Jones lived before the war and where she was married, the battle flag she stitched together was kept by the Blair family through the rest of the war. Blair's mother, sixty-year-old Martha C. Blair, was the one who most likely stitched the battle honors, "Shiloh" and "Perryville," on the flag.[25]

Epilogue

The Fifth Company fought gallantly through the Battle of Murfreesboro in December 1862 and early January 1863. It spent the winter with the Army of the Tennessee at Tullahoma, Tennessee, and in September 1863 fought for two days in the Battle of Chickamauga in north Georgia.[1]

One of the company's most remembered artillery duels occurred at Chickamauga. On the morning of September 19, 1863, Captain Slocumb posted two of his rifled guns on a bluff above Glass's Mill; he crossed Chickamauga Creek with his remaining four smooth-bore guns. As his men were unlimbering those smooth-bores, they came under heavy enemy fire. No sooner had Slocumb's cannoneers silenced the enemy fire than eleven Federal rifled guns opened up on the Fifth Company's exposed guns. Some of the Fifth Company's guns and limbers were severely damaged and had to be withdrawn. Seven horses were killed. Lt. Thomas Blair—the one who took Mary Henry Lyon Jones's flag to his family in Mobile for safekeeping—and six cannoneers were killed; four men were wounded. Blair's remains were returned to Mobile, Alabama, where they were buried in the cemetery of his family's Spring Hill farm, where Blair was born.[2]

The Fifth Company and the Louisiana brigade, commanded by Col. Randall Lee Gibson after Gen. Adams received three wounds, fought desperately through the second day of battle at Chickamauga. It followed the army to Chattanooga, where it defended the heights of Missionary Ridge only to be forced to give them up on November 28.[3]

Falling all the way back to Dalton, Georgia, the Fifth Company fought through the heartbreaking struggle, resisting the relentless approach to Atlanta of Maj. Gen. William T. Sherman's armies. After Atlanta was given up, the Fifth Company followed Maj. Gen. John Bell Hood's Army of Tennessee in its desperate campaign to retake Tennessee in the fall of 1864. From the bloody fields at Franklin on November 28 to the frozen hills south of Nashville on December 12, the Fifth Company fought on from one defeat to another.[4]

Incredibly, the Fifth Company at the last defended—and then surrendered at—Mobile, Alabama, in April 1865. There its first battle flag had been kept and there its maker had resided and was wed before the war. The last defenses Captain Slocumb's men held at Mobile were named "Fort Blair" in honor of the beloved lieutenant who died at Chickamauga and whose family guarded the battery's first flag made by Mary Henry Lyon Jones.[5]

The flag had come full circle. Its story began in Mobile and ended there.

Mary Henry Lyon Jones lived through the rest of the war in Richmond, though she made frequent visits to Mobile—often, it seems, because of frail health. While in Richmond, she worked at Robertson Hospital near her home. When her uncle, Francis Strother Lyon, was elected to the Confederate Congress in 1862, he lived at the Sixth Street home of Mary and her husband. When Richmond fell to General Grant's forces in April 1865, Lyon was with Mary and James.[6]

Those last days before the fall of Richmond were very difficult; Mary was seven months pregnant when the city fell. On April 2, 1865, Mary accompanied her close friend, Amelia Gorgas, wife of Brig. Gen. Josiah Gorgas, to Amelia's sister's home. Earlier in the day, while at St. Paul's Church, they heard that Gen. Robert E. Lee's lines had been broken at Petersburg and his army was evacuating Richmond. While Mary was seated on the sofa with Amelia Gorgas's sister, a "fragment of a shell crashed through the window and passed within a few inches of their heads." Fires raged all over the city. The women threw wet blankets over the roof to protect it from the burning debris that rained down.[7]

Mary Henry Lyon Jones's uncle, Francis Strother Lyon, a carte de visite *photograph.* (Courtesy of the Alabama Department of Archives and History, Montgomery, Alabama)

There was "wild confusion on the streets." The starving people of the city had broken into houses, warehouses, and commissary stores, looking for food and clothing. Starving animals were everywhere. Over Church Hill, just beyond the spire of St. James Church, Mary could see the Federal troops. Recalled Amelia Gorgas: "The brilliant uniforms of the officers and men and the sleek, prancing horses formed a painful contrast to our ragged and shoeless braves and their half-starved animals."[8]

Mary, Amelia Gorgas, and Amelia's sister bravely stepped outside and found the headquarters of Maj. Gen. Edward O. C. Ord, who had been a classmate of General Gorgas at West Point. Ord was then commander of the Army of the James and the Department of North Carolina. The three frightened women struggled to get into the building. An aid stopped them and then, in the words of Amelia Gorgas, "[caught] a glimpse of the pale and beautiful face of [Mary Henry Lyon Jones] and invited us with some solicitude to be seated." In minutes, the aid ordered a "tall Prussian soldier" to accompany the women to the home where they were all staying to protect them. Recalled Amelia Gorgas after the war:

> After our little ones were asleep, we three . . . tired, heart-broken women sat bewailing the terrible misfortune that had befallen our beloved city. We tried to comfort ourselves by saying in low tones . . . that the capital was only moved temporarily to Danville, that General Lee would make a stand and repulse the daring enemy, and that he should yet win the battle and the day. Alas! Alas for our hopes![9]

Mary Henry Lyon Jones gave birth to a daughter, Mary Morris Jones, on June 1, 1865. She would marry Confederate veteran David Gardiner Tyler, the son of Pres. John Tyler and his second wife, Julia Gardiner Tyler. Gardiner had entered Washington College in Lexington, Virginia (now Washington and Lee University) before the war, but left in 1862 to join the Rockbridge Artillery. He served in that famous command all the way to Appomattox, where he surrendered on April 9, 1865. He returned to Washington College in 1866 and entered its law school. At that time, Robert E. Lee was president of the college.

It was Lee who merged the Lexington, Virginia, law school of Judge John Brockenborough into the college in 1867 and Lee who signed Tyler's diploma. A lawyer in Richmond, a state legislator, and a circuit judge, Tyler was elected to Congress in 1894, about the time he and Mary Morris Jones were married. Four children would be born to the Tylers: Mary Lyon Tyler in 1895, Margaret Gardiner Tyler in 1897, David Gardiner Tyler in 1899, and James Alfred Jones Tyler in 1902. The Tylers were members of St. Paul's Episcopal Church in Richmond; there, they were often joined by Mary Henry Lyon Jones and James Alfred Jones.[10]

Mary Henry Lyon Jones died in Mobile, Alabama, on March 30, 1886, after a long illness. Her funeral was held at St. James Episcopal Church in Richmond. Her husband, James Alfred Jones, died not long thereafter. Both are buried near the plots of President John Tyler and the Tyler family members in Hollywood Cemetery in Richmond. Though nothing on the tombstone denotes her contributions to the war effort, Mary Henry Lyon Jones stitched together the first Confederate St. Andrew's Cross battle flag ever made, a flag borne out of nothing more than military necessity.[11]

The St. Andrew's Cross battle flag became the single most noted emblem of the Confederacy and, perhaps, the American Civil War. More than one million lives were lost fighting to defend—or crush—what that emblem represented. Mary Henry Lyon Jones actually stitched together the first flag by hand; it was borne through the battles of Shiloh and Perryville. When Mary Henry Lyon Jones made that flag, the Confederate government was not only yet to approve the design but also totally unaware that the flag was even being made for the army. Using the flag Mary Henry Lyon Jones stitched together, the first mass production of such flags was accomplished using the sewing skills of hundreds of ladies like Mary, organized by church groups and altar guilds in Richmond, Virginia, all completely without the authority—or even the knowledge—of the Confederate government. It is hard to imagine that such a famous battle emblem had such tender beginnings.

Abbreviations

ESBL   Elinor S. Brockenbrough Memorial Library
H-TML   Howard-Tilton Memorial Library
LHAP   Louisiana Historical Association Papers
LL   Lewis Leigh, Jr.
LWK   Lon W. Keim, MD
MMB   Mary Morris Booth
MOC   Museum of the Confederacy
PBSHS   Perryville Battlefield State Historic Site
TU   Tulane University
VSL   Virginia State Library
WML   William M. Lyon, Jr.

Notes

Chapter One

1. *Charleston Daily Courier*, December 18, 1860.

2. Charles H. Lesser, *Relic of the Lost Cause: The Story of South Carolina's Ordinance of Secession* (Columbia, South Carolina Department of Archives and History, 1996) 2-6; *Charleston Mercury*, December 20, 1860.

3. Lesser, *Relic of the Lost Cause*, 2; *Charleston Daily Courier*, December 21, 1860. The original flag that hung behind the president's chair at the secession convention is in the collections of the South Carolina Department of Archives and History in Columbia.

4. Lesser, *Relic of the Lost Cause*, 2.

5. *Ibid.*, 8-9; Kenneth Severens, *Charleston Antebellum Architecture and Civic Destiny.* (Knoxville: University of Tennessee Press, 1988) 217-220.

6. *Charleston Mercury*, December 3, 1860. A marvelous example of a South Carolina Lone Star flag may be seen in the collections of the Confederate Museum in Charleston.

7. *Charleston Mercury*, November 10, 1860; *Charleston Mercury*, November 14, 1860.

8. S.A. Cunningham, ed., "The First Confederate Flag," *Confederate Veteran*, 11 (1903) 225.

9. *Charleston Mercury*, December 6, 1860.

10. *Charleston Daily Courier*, December 21, 1860.

11. *New York Herald*, December 25, 1860; *Illustrated London News*, February 2, 1861.

12. *Frank Leslie's Illustrated Newspaper*, February 2, 1861.

13. Devereaux D. Cannon, Jr., *The Flags of the Confederacy, An Illustrated History* (Memphis: St. Luke's Press, 1988) 34-35.

14. David M. Potter, *The Impending Crisis, 1848-1861* (New York: Harper & Row Pub., 1976) 498-99.

15. Cannon, *The Flags of the Confederacy*, 38. The Alabama Secession Flag is in the collections of the Alabama Department of Archives and History in Montgomery.

16. *Ibid.*, 36-43. The provisional flag of Florida between January 13, 1861, and September 13, 1861, consisted of thirteen red and white stripes and a blue field with a large, white, five-pointed star. Louisiana adopted a flag similar to Florida's on February 11, 1861, except it had three red stripes, four blue stripes and six white stripes; its large single star in a red field was yellow. Texas adopted a naval ensign identical to the Florida flag. The secession flag adopted after Louisiana seceded from the Union on January 26, 1861, is in the collection of Lon W. Keim, MD, Omaha, Nebraska.

17. Charles Robert Lee, Jr., *The Confederate Constitutions* (Chapel Hill: The University of North Carolina Press, 1863) 62-122. The Confederate Constitutions, indeed, copied many of the essential features of the United States Constitution. The rights guaranteed in the first eight amendments to the United States Constitution were set forth in the body of the Confederate provisional and first and second Constitutions. In addition, the Confederate Constitutions, among other things, limited the president to one six-year term, imbedded the philosophy of state sovereignty, gave the president the line-item veto, and mandated that appropriation bills specify the amount and purpose of the appropriations. And, apart from the incorporation of provisions protecting the institution of slavery, the Confederate Constitutions read much like the United States Constitution.

18. William Warren Rogers, Jr., *Confederate Homefront: Montgomery During the Civil War* (Tuscaloosa: The University of Alabama Press, 1999) 1-2.

19. *Charleston Daily Courier*, May 14, 1861; *Journal of the Congress of the Confederate States of America (1861)*, 5 vols. (Washington: Government Printing Office, 1904) 1:40, 208-

13, 242-43; Emory M. Thomas, *The Confederate Nation, 1861-1865* (New York: Harper & Row Pub., 1979) 60-62; Cannon, *The Flags of the Confederacy*, 7. Because Davis was still *en route* to Montgomery from his home in Vicksburg, Mississippi, Alexander H. Stephens of Georgia was sworn into the office of vice president on February 11. Davis and Stephens had been unanimously elected to serve as president and vice president respectively by the Provisional Confederate Congress.

20. *Charleston Mercury*, February 11, 1861.

21. *Charleston Daily Courier*, February 15, 1861.

22. "Nicola Marschall," *Wikipedia,* last modified March 17, 2013, http://en.wikipedia.org/wiki/Nicola_Marschall.

23. Cannon, *The Flags of the Confederacy*, 9.

24. *Charleston Mercury*, March 6, 1861.

25. Alfred Roman, *The Military Operations of General Beauregard In The War Between the States, 1861-1865*, 2 vols. (New York: Harper & Brothers, 1884) I:48. The Stars and Bars flag that was first flown over Fort Sumter is in the collections of the Confederate Museum in Charleston. The palmetto flag that flew over Fort Sumter with the Stars and Bars may be seen in the collections of the Fort Sumter National Historic Site in Charleston Harbor.

26. Richard N. Current, ed., *Encyclopedia of the Confederacy*, 4 vols. (New York: Simon & Schuster, 1993) 3:1038.

27. *Charleston Mercury*, December 28, 1860.

28. "Saltire," *Wikipedia*, last modified September 15, 2013, https://en.wikipedia.org/wiki/Saltire.

29. Cannon, *Flags of the Confederacy*, 27-28. For a discussion of the origins of the St. Andrew's Cross, see John W. Coski, *The Confederate Battle Flag: America's Most Embattled Emblem.* (Cambridge, MA: Belknap Press of Harvard University Press, 2005) 4-6.

30. J.B. Walton to G.T. Beauregard, January 13, 1872, in Roman, *Military Operations of General Beauregard*, I:483; J.B. Walton to G.T. Beauregard, January 30, 1872, LHAP, H-TML, TU.

31. *Ibid.*

Chapter Two

1. *The War of the Rebellion: A Compilation of the Official*

Records of the Union and Confederate Armies, 128 vols. (Washington, DC, 1880-1901) Series I (hereinafter "*OR*,"), 2:437, 568-69. Beauregard was able to report 21,863 officers and men in his Army of the Potomac. Johnston was unable to provide a count of the strength of his regiments; the Army of the Shenandoah must have totaled in excess of 15,000, according to Beauregard's report.

2. Ezra J. Warner, *Generals in Gray: Lives of the Confederate Commanders* (Baton Rouge: Louisiana State University Press, 1959) 22-23.

3. *OR*, 2:440.

4. *Ibid.*, 473; Warner, *Generals in Gray*, 161-62.

5. *OR*, 2:306, 309, 317; Ezra J. Warner, *Generals in Blue: Lives of the Union Commanders*, (Baton Rouge: Louisiana State University Press, 1964) 297-99.

6. *OR*, 2:473, 985.

7. *Ibid.*, 469-70, 479-80.

8. *Ibid.*, 480.

9. *Ibid.*, 318, 473-74, 480.

10. *Ibid.*, 318.

11. *Ibid.*, 318-19, 474.

12. *Ibid.*, 474, 559.

13. *Ibid.*, 474, 559, 493-94.

14. *Ibid.*, 319-20, 481-82; William C. Davis, *Battle at Bull Run: A History of the First Major Campaign of the Civil War*. (New York: Doubleday & Co., 1977) 204-5.

15. *OR*, 2:475-76, 492-93.

16. *Ibid.*, 319.

17. *Ibid.*, 320, 490-93.

18. *Ibid.*, 490-93; John Brighton Brock, "Symbols of a Nation: The First Flag of the Confederacy was Made in Montgomery," *Alabama Living* (March 2011) 17.

19. *OR*, 2:495; Davis, *Battle of Bull Run*, 199.

20. Warner, *Generals in Gray*, 79-80.

21. *OR*, 2:557

22. *Ibid.*, 82-83.

23. Jubal A. Early to Jefferson Davis, December 30, 1878, LHAP, H-TML, TU.

24. *OR*, 2:557.

25. *Ibid.*, 541.

26. Thomas Jordan to G.T. Beauregard, January 28, 1872, in Roman, *Military Operations of General Beauregard*, I:486-87.

27. Joseph E. Johnston, *Narrative of Military Operations, Directed, During the Late War Between the States*, (New York: D. Appleton and Company, 1874) 60-70.

28. *OR*, 2:477, 503.

29. *Ibid.*, 327, 477.

Chapter Three

1. Johnston, *Narrative of Military Operations*, 60; *OR*, 2:504.

2. John Milner Associates, Inc., *Fairfax County Civil War Sites Inventory* (Fairfax County, VA: Fairfax County Board of Supervisors, August 2002) http://www.fairfaxcounty.gov/parks/resource-management/downloads/civilwarinventory.pdf, 18-19.

3. Roman, *Military Operations of General Beauregard*, I:136; Warner, *Generals in Gray*, 280-81.

4. *OR*, 2:475; Karl Reinee, "The House of Shattered Dreams," September 29, 2004, http://www.connectionnewspapers.com/news/2004/sep/29/the-house-of-shattered-dreams/; Roman, *Military Operations of General Beauregard*, I:104; Davis, *Battle of Bull Run*, 200.

5. G.T. Beauregard, "The First Battle of Bull Run," Robert Underwood Johnson and Clarence Clough Buel, eds., *Battles and Leaders of the Civil War*, 4 vols. (New York: Thomas Yoseloff), I:201; Davis, *Battle at Bull Run,* 57, 262. All of Beauregard's dispatches and letters from the McLean House were noted as having been sent from "Manassas."

6. *OR*, 2:473, 763, 766.

7. G.T. Beauregard to William Porcher Miles, August 27, 1861, ESBL, MOC. Moise is quoted in Robert E. Bonner, *Colors and Blood: Flag Passions of the Confederate South* (Princeton: Princeton University Press) 101-2.

8. The letter is not still extant, but General Beauregard refers to it in G.T. Beauregard to William Porcher Miles, September 4, 1861, and G.T. Beauregard to Joseph E. Johnston, September 5, 1861, in Roman, *Military Operations of General Beauregard*, I:482.

9. G.T. Beauregard to William Porcher Miles, September 4, 1861, in Roman, *Military Operations of General Beauregard*, I:483. The letter was written from Beauregard's headquarters at "Manassas," overlooking Bull Run and the Confederate camps west and south of Centreville.

10. G.T. Beauregard to Joseph E. Johnston, September 5, 1861, in Roman, *Military Operations of General Beauregard*, I:482. The letter was written from Beauregard's headquarters at "Manassas," overlooking Bull Run and the Confederate camps west and south of Centreville.

11. Joseph E. Johnston to G.T. Beauregard, January 16, 1872, in Roman, *Military Operations of General Beauregard*, I:484.

12. Colin McRae Selph to Col. J.A. Chalaron, July 25, 1905, LHAP, H-TML, TU.

13. *Ibid*., Joseph E. Johnston to G.T. Beauregard, January 16, 1872, in Roman, *Military Operations of General Beauregard*, I:484.

14. Beauregard, "The First Battle of Bull Run," 201.

15. J.B. Walton to G.T. Beauregard, January 13, 1872, in Roman, *Military Operations of General Beauregard*, I:483; Joseph F. Johnston to G.T. Beauregard, January 16, 1872, in Roman, *Military Operations of General Beauregard,* I:484.

16. Miller Associates, *Fairfax County Civil War Sites Inventory*, 16-17; Joseph E. Johnston to G.T. Beauregard, January 16, 1872, in Roman, *Military Operations of General Beauregard*, I:484.

17. Joseph E. Johnston to G.T. Beauregard, January 16, 1872, in Roman, *Military Operations of General Beauregard*, I:484; G.T. Beauregard to G.H. Preble, January 24, 1872, LHAP, H-TML, TU; *New York Times*, February 17, 1872; General Gustavus W. Smith recalled a conference at Fairfax Court House about the flag in a letter to G.T. Beauregard, January 15, 1872, LHAP, H-TML, TU; General W.L. Cabell also recalled being summoned to a meeting at Fairfax Court House with Generals Johnston, Beauregard, and Smith, but Johnston, Beauregard, and Smith did not recall Cabell being in attendance. Cabell was not there; rather, he was summoned to Johnston's headquarters at Centreville as the army was returning there. W.L. Cabell, "True History of Our Battle Flag," *Confederate Veteran*, 11 (1903) 339-40; Colin McRae

Selph to Col. J.A. Chalaron, July 25, 1905, LHAP, H-TML, TU; See also: Charleton McCarthy, "Origin of the Confederate Battle Flag," *Southern Historical Society Papers*, 8 (1880) 197-99.

18. Miller Associates, *Fairfax County Civil War Sites Inventory*, 18; Johnston, *Narrative of Military Operations*, 77.

19. Colin McRae Selph to Col. J.A. Chalaron, July 25, 1905, LHAP, H-TML, TU; Warner, *Generals in Gray*, 41-42.

20. Joseph E. Johnston to G.T. Beauregard, January 16, 1872, in Roman, *Military Operations of General Beauregard*, I:484.

21. *Ibid.*

22. *Ibid.*

Chapter Four

1. W.L. Cabell to Col. J.A. Chalaron, August 5, 1903, Colin McRae Selph to Col. J.A. Chalaron, July 25, 1905, LHAP, H-TML, TU; Robert E.L. Krick, *Staff Officers in Gray: Biographical Record of the Staff Officers in the Army of Northern Virginia,* (Chapel Hill, University of North Carolina Press, 2009), 263.

2. Colin McRae Selph to Col. J.A. Chalaron, July 25, 1905, LHAP, H-TML, TU; Current, *Encyclopedia of the Confederacy*, III:1106.

3. Colin McRae Selph to Col. J.A. Chalaron, July 25, 1905, LHAP, H-TML, TU; *Richmond City Business Directory, 1860,* n.p., 7-8, at http://www.mdgorman.com.

4. Colin McRae Selph to Col. J.A. Chalaron, July 25, 1905, LHAP, H-TML, TU; *Richmond City Business Directory, 1860,* 2.7; Fonda G. Thomsen to Lon W. Keim, M.D., "Analysis Report," April 20, 1996, LWK. Thomsen, a nationally renowned authority on flags, examined the battle flag made by Mary Henry Lyon Jones. She recorded meticulous findings and notes about its construction and use.

5. Colin McRae Selph to Col. J.A. Chalaron, July 25, 1905, LHAP, H-TML, TU; *In Memoriam, Mary Henry Jones* (died March 20, 1886), n.p., n.d. VSL.

6. "Francis Strother Lyon," *Wikipedia,* last modified March 16, 2013, http://en.wikipedia.org/wiki/Francis_Strother_Lyon; "My Dear Parent" from Mary, July 28, 1859, WML.

7. *In Memoriam, Mary Henry Jones*, VSL.

8. *Ibid.*; http://penelope.uchicago.edu/Thayer/E/Gazetteer/Places/America/United_States/Army/USMA/Cullums_Register/903*.html; *James Alfred Jones L.L.D.* typescript, n.p., n.d., VSL.

9. Cynthia Miller Leonard, compiler, *The General Assembly of Virginia*, July 30, 1619–January 11, 1978 (Richmond: Virginia State Library, 1978) 440, 457, 462; John Herbert Claiborne, MA, MD, *Petersburg in the 1850's*, Marvin T. Boyhill, III, ed. (Petersburg: Appomattox Iron Works, 1993) 26-27; Lyon Gardiner Tyler, LLD, *Encyclopedia of Virginia Biography* (New York: Lewis Historical Pub. Co., 1915) 299; *James Alfred Jones, LLD*, typescript, VSL.

10. *James Alfred Jones L.L.D.* typescript, VSL; "Dear Mary" from "Devoted Husband," May 24, 1862, "My Dear Mary" from "Your ever devoted husband," May 25, 1862, MMB.

11. Printer, *The City Intelligencer or Stranger's Guide* (Richmond: McFarlane & Ferguson, Printers, 1862), 4. In that document Congressman Francis Strother Lyon of Alabama is noted as residing at the home of "J. Alfred Jones, Sixth Street, between Franklin and Main."

12. War Department, *Regulations of the Army of the Confederate States*, 1863 (Richmond: J.W. Randolph, 1863) §§ 892, 988-92, 1161-62.

13. *Richmond Dispatch*, October 12, 1861. An article entitled "Ladies' Hospitals in Richmond for the Sick and Soldiers" on page 2 lists sixteen hospitals; Printer, *The City Intelligencer or Stranger's Guide,* lists fifty hospitals in the City of Richmond by 1862.

14. Elizabeth Dabney Coleman, "The Captain Was a Lady." *Virginia Cavalcade*, 6 (Summer 1956-Spring 1957) 35-41; *Richmond Enquirer*, June 18, 1861; *Richmond Enquirer*, September 17, 1861; *Richmond Enquirer*, September 25, 1861. Sally Tompkins would be commissioned a captain in the Confederate cavalry on September 9, 1861, so she could keep her hospital open after the Confederate Congress required commissioned officers in the army to oversee all military hospitals. Tompkins was the only woman actually commissioned as an officer in the Confederate army.

15. Wadesboro *North Carolina Argus*, June 19, 1862; *Richmond Enquirer*, October 5, 1861; C. Van Woodward, *Mary Chestnut's Civil War* (New Haven: Yale University Press, 1981), 143, 149, 158, 161, 164.

16. Krick, *Staff Officers in Gray*, 205.

17. Thompson, "Analysis Report."

18. Colin McRae Selph to Col. J.A. Chalaron, July 25, 1905, LHAP, H-TML, TU.

19. *Ibid.*; *Richmond Times Dispatch*, June 16, 1912.

20. Mrs. Burton Harrison, *Recollections Grave and Gay*. (New York: Charles Scribner's Sons, 1911) 1-45.

21. *Ibid.*, Constance Cary Harrison, "Virginia Scenes in '61," in Robert Underwood Johnson and Clarence Clough Buell, eds. *Battles and Leaders of the Civil War*, 4 vols. (New York: Thomas Yoseloff, 1956), I:160-61.

22. Harrison, *Recollections Grave and Gay*, 46; "Virginia Scenes in '61," 163.

23. Louise Pecquet du Bellet, et al., *Some Prominent Virginia Families*, 4 vols. (Lynchburg: J.P. Bell Co., 1907), II:81, 88-90; Roger D. Cary, "Belle Run," *Baltimore Sun*, October 25, 2000.

24. Henry Kyd Douglas, *I Rode With Stonewall* (Chapel Hill: The University of North Carolina Press, 1940) 271, 325.

25. Harrison, *Recollections Grave and Gay*, 56-58; Walter S. Griggs, Jr., "The Cary Invincibles," http://trendmag2.trendoffset.com/display_article.php?id=686106.

26. Harrison, *Recollections Grave and Gay*, 57.

27. *Ibid.*, 58; http://www.csadealer.com/items-for-sale. Patricia A. Kaufman, a stamp and envelope dealer, posted an envelope addressed to "Hetty Cary care [of] Dr. Thos. T. Slaughter, Orange Ct. House, Virginia," illustrating her lengthy visits there.

28. Harrison, *Recollections Grave and Gay*, 47.

29. Brig. Gen. G. Moxley Sorrel, C.S.A., *Recollections of a Confederate Staff Officer*, Bell Irvin Wiley, ed. (Jackson: McCowat-Mercer Press, 1958) 46.

30. Harrison, *Recollections Grave and Gay*, 59.

31. *Ibid.*, 59-60; Krick, *Staff Officers in Gray*, 67, 162-63; Robert K. Krick, *Lee's Colonels: A Biographical Register of the Field Officers of the Army of Northern Virginia*. (Dayton: Press of Morningside, 1979), 261; Current, *Encyclopedia of the Confederacy*, I, 199-201, 354-55.

32. Francis W. Dawson, "Letters of a British Officer in the Confederacy," American Civil War Forum, http://www.

americancivilwarforum.com/letters-of-francis-w.-dawson-british-officer-in-the-confederacy-1353418.html; Griggs, "The Cary Invincibles;" Colin McRae Selph to Col. J.A. Chalaron, July 25, 1905, LHAP, H-TML, TU.

33. Colin McRae Selph to Col. J.A. Chalaron, July 25, 1905, LHAP, H-TML, TU.

34. It would have taken at least 400 women working in shifts, around the clock, to make 120 flags in less than one month. Editor, "The Confederate Flag," *Southern Historical Society Papers*, 8 (1880), 155-57.

35. The flags made by Caroline Beauregard and Kitty Hill are in the collections of the Museum of the Confederacy in Richmond, Virginia. There the provenance accompanying the flags is preserved.

36. All of the known flags made by the ladies of Richmond are made from two double-strips of silk; usually one of the pieces is sixteen and one-half inches wide. Most have gold fringe; some have gold or white borders. The stars are mostly painted on the saltires.

37. Editor, "The Confederate Flag," 155-57.

Chapter Five

1. Miller Associates, *Fairfax County Civil War Sites Inventory*, 20.

2. *Ibid.*; McHenry Howard, *Recollections of a Maryland Confederate Soldier and Staff Officer Under Johnston, Jackson and Lee*. (Dayton: Press of Morningside Bookshop, 1975) 61.

3. Augustus D. Dickert, *History of Kershaw's Brigade*. (Dayton: Press of Morningside Bookshop, 1976) 83-84.

4. Miller Associates, *Fairfax County Civil War Sites Inventory*, 15, 19; *Map Showing the Confederate Encampments Around Centreville, 1861-1862*. Collection of Manassas Battlefield Park, NPS, Manassas, Virginia.

5. Joseph Mills Hanson, *Bull Run Remembers: History, Traditions and Landmarks of the Manassas (Bull Run) Campaign Before Washington 1861-1862*. (Manassas, VA: National Capital Publishers, 1957) 39.

6. Johnston, *Narrative of Military Operations*, 79.

7. W.H. Morgan, *Personal Reminiscences of the War of 1861-5*. (Lynchburg: J.P. Bell Co., Inc., 1911) 94.

8. As the flags were presented to the regiments of the army on

November 28, Lieutenant Selph would have had to have brought them to Centreville just before then.

9. Sorrel, *Recollections of a Confederate Staff Officer*, 28-29.

10. Current, *Encyclopedia of the Confederacy*, II:870-71; *Military Operations of General Beauregard*, I:481; Original *General Order No. 75, November 28, 1861* in the collections of Lewis Leigh, Jr., Leesburg, Virginia. The order is signed in brown ink by Thomas Jordan as adjutant general; *Richmond Whig*, December 4, 1861.

11. *Richmond Whig*, December 4, 1861.

12. J.W. Reid, *History of the Fourth Regiment of South Carolina Volunteers*. (Dayton: Press of Morningside Bookshop, 1975) 60.

13. Sam Payne to Cousin (Mollie), December 1, 1861, "To Mollie" Letters, ESBL, MOC.

14. Susan Leigh Blackford, comp., *Memoirs of Life In and Out of the Army in Virginia During the War Between the States*, 2 vols. (Lynchburg: J.P. Bell Co., 1894) I:97.

15. "Confederate Battle Flags' History–1 (U.S.)," Museum of the Confederacy, last modified October 15, 2010, http://www.crwflags.com/fotw/flags/us-csah.html. The silk did not last long; many of the flags issued to the troops on November 28, 1861, and the weeks thereafter were reduced to tatters by the summer of 1862. Some, however, stayed with their regiments until the ensuing winter of 1862-63. By the spring of 1862 there were very limited issues of replacement flags. The Richmond Clothing Depot, established in late 1861 for the manufacture of uniforms, shoes, accoutrements, and flags, began to manufacture replacement St. Andrew's Cross battle flags. Most were made of bunting; some were made of wool. Before the end of the war, there would be seven wool bunting issues of such flags.

16. Harrison, *Recollections Grave and Gay*, 61; C. Van Woodward, *Mary Chesnut's Civil War*, 539. While talking about Hetty Cary, Constance Cary pointed to Maj. Gen. J.E.B. Stuart's collar emblems and said those words to Mary Chesnut, the diarist.

17. Harrison, *Recollections Grave and Gay,* 61; C.C. Harrison to Col. J.E. Graybill, March 21, 1908, LHAP, EH-TML, TU.

18. Harrison, *Recollections Grave and Gay*, 61.

19. *Ibid*., 62-63.

20. *Ibid.*, 61. The facts surrounding Hetty and Jennie Cary's travels to Charlottesville are interesting. Constance Cary wrote that they "went to Albemarle," meaning Albemarle County, Virginia. The letter Jennie Cary wrote to General Beauregard enclosing her flag was written from the "University of Virginia." It has often been noted that they visited "friends" in Charlottesville. A stamp and envelope dealer, Patricia A. Kaufman, recently posted two letters addressed to Hetty Cary: one of them "care [of] Dr. Thos. T. Slaughter, Orange Ct. House, Virginia," heretofore noted, and the other "care [of] Mrs. Sydney Carr, University of Va." The second envelope solved the mystery. Mrs. Sydney Carr was the widow of Dabney S. Carr, the brother of Hetty and Jennie Cary's mother. Dabney S. Carr's grandfather, Dabney Carr, is buried at Monticello. Mrs. Sydney Carr owned a boarding house that was located on "Carr's Hill," the present site of the president's home at the University of Virginia. It stands across from the famed Rotunda on the campus. Formerly known as Brockenbrough Hill, the boarding house on that site was first owned by Lucy Brockenbrough, widow of Arthur S. Brockenbrough. The property was sold, as a result of a lawsuit to collect debts, to a professor at the university who, in turn, sold the property to the university. It was Thomas Jefferson Randolph, the rector of the university and kinsman to Dabney S. Carr and his wife, who sold it to Carr's widow in 1854 shortly after Carr died. Mrs. Carr was already living in the house when she bought it. From that time forward the site was always known as Carr's Hill, and is so today. See: "Jefferson and the 19th Century, Carr's Hill Centennial Celebration," University of Virginia, last modified August 27, 2009, http://www.virginia.edu/carrshill/jefferson.html.

21. The original letters from Jennie Cary to General Beauregard, dated December 12, 1861, and from General Beauregard to Jennie Cary, dated December 15, 1861, are in the collections of Lewis Leigh, Jr., Leesburg, Virginia; Colin McRae Selph to J.A. Chalaron, July 25, 1905, LHAP, H-TML, TU. Selph recalled Banks being the courier.

22. C.C. Harrison to Col. J.E. Graybill, March 21, 1908, LHAP, H-TML, TU. Constance wrote to Colonel Graybill to let him know that the flag was returned to her. The silk flags made by Hetty and Constance Cary are in the collections of the Museum of the

Confederacy in Richmond, Virginia. The flag made by Jennie Cary is in the collections of the Louisiana State Museum in Baton Rouge, Louisiana.

The Cary girls remained in the spotlight through the rest of the war. They would be seen often at Richmond functions. Constance met Burton Harrison, a private secretary for Jefferson Davis, and actually helped win his release from Fort Delaware prison at the end of the war. Constance and Burton were married in Westchester County, New York, in 1867. One of their children, Fairfax Harrison, became president of the Southern Railway Company; another, Francis Burton Harrison, became governor general of the Philippines. Constance became a published author of many books and articles. She died in Washington, DC, in 1920 and is buried in Ivy Hill Cemetery in Alexandria, Virginia.

Hetty Cary fell in love with the dashing Brig. Gen. John Pegram during the war. On January 19, 1865, they were married in St. Paul's Episcopal Church in one of the most celebrated of all war-time Confederate weddings. Sadly, on February 6, eighteen days after the wedding, General Pegram was killed in action at the Battle of Hatcher's Run outside Petersburg. Hetty was in Pegram's headquarters in Petersburg at the time and rode in the freight car with her husband's remains back to Richmond, where Pegram was buried in Hollywood Cemetery. After staying with her mother-in-law for an extended period of time, Hetty returned to Baltimore. While traveling in Europe, she met Henry Newell Martin, a physiologist and professor at Johns Hopkins University. They were married in 1879. Hetty died at her home in Baltimore on September 27, 1892, and is buried in the St. Thomas Episcopal Church Cemetery at Owings Mills, Baltimore, Maryland, alongside her husband and parents.

Jennie Cary never married. She died on November 16, 1925, and is also buried in the Cary plot at St. Thomas Episcopal Church. "Constance Cary Harrison," *Wikipedia,* last modified August 13, 2013, http://en.wikipedia.org/wiki/Constance_Cary_Harrison; "Hetty Cary, JHBL Family Genealogy," http://www.latrobefamily.com/genealogy/getperson.php?personID=I5349&tree=mytree; du Bellet, *Some Prominent Virginia Families*, II:81, 88-90; Cary, "Belle Run."

Chapter Six

1. Presentation to the president and members of the Association of the Army of the Tennessee, Colin McRae Selph to J.A. Chalaron, July 25, 1905 and Sumpter Turner to Mr. J.E. Grayhill, April 25, 1908. LHAP, H-TML, TU. Those documents firmly establish that Mary Henry Lyon Jones's flag was given to Major Walton and he, in turn, gave it to the Fifth Company of the Washington Artillery of New Orleans. See also: *New Orleans Daily Picayune*, n.d., LHAP, H-TML, TU.

2. Warner, *Generals in Gray*, 159-60; Roman, *Military Operations of General Beauregard*, I:243-44.

3. Nathanial Cheairs Hughes, Jr., *The Pride of the Confederate Artillery: The Washington Artillery in the Army of the Tennessee.* (Baton Rouge: Louisiana State University Press, 1997) 4-6, 316.

4. *Ibid.*, 12-20, 340-41.

5. *Ibid.*, 5, 9, 298-99, 316, 345-46.

6. *Ibid.*, 7, 22, 283-351; *OR*, 10(1):496, 513.

7. *New Orleans Daily Picayune*, March 3, 1862; Hughes, *Pride of the Confederate Artillery*, 12.

8. *OR*, 10(1):494-96, 514-15; Warner, *Generals in Gray*, 30-31.

9. P.D. Stevenson, "The Fifth Company, Washington Artillery," *New Orleans Times-Picayune*, March 10, 1902.

10. Howard Michael Madaus and Robert D. Needham, *The Battle Flags of the Confederate Army of Tennessee.* (Milwaukee: Milwaukee Public Museum, 1976) 21-27, 49-58.

11. *OR*, 10(1):100-11, 385.

12. *Ibid.*, 513-14.

13. *Ibid.*, 278-79.

14. *Ibid.*, 387.

15. *Ibid.*, 453-56, 480; Warner, *Generals in Gray*, 104-5.

16. Warner, *Generals in Gray*, 265-66; *OR*, 10(1):471-72.

17. "The Fifth Company, Washington Artillery." *New Orleans Times-Picayune*, March 10, 1902.

18. Warner, *Generals in Blue*, 51-52.

19. *OR*, 10(1):480-81, 514-15.

20. A. Gordon Bakewell, "Shiloh," typescript, LHAP, H-TML, TU.

21. *OR,* 10(1): 480-81, 514-15.

Chapter Seven

1. *OR*, 16(1):1023, 1088-90.

2. Warner, *Generals in Gray*, 1-2.

3. *OR*, 16(1):1122-24; Warner, *Generals in Gray*, 104-5.

4. *OR*, 16(1):1119-24; Warner, *Generals in Gray*, 124-25.

5. *Ibid.*, 16(1):1024.

6. *Ibid.*, 16(1):1090-92, 1096, 1098-110.

7. *Ibid.*, 16(1):1092, 1110-18.

8. *Ibid.*, 16(1):1120-23.

9. *Ibid,.* 16(1):1044-49; Warner, *Generals in Blue*, 412-13.

10. *OR,* 16(1):1039-44, 1110-11, 1113-19, 1062-68; Warner, *Generals in Blue*, 496-97.

11. *OR,* 16(1):1039-42, 1045-46; Sam Watkins, *Company Aytch: A Side Show of the Big Show*. Bell Irvin Wiley, ed. (Jackson, McCowat Mercer Press, 1952) 82.

12. Warner, *Generals in Blue*, 413; Watkins, *Company Aytch*, 82.

13. Thomas D. Head, *Campaigns and Battles of the Sixteenth Tennessee Infantry* (Nashville: Cumberland Presbyterian Pub., 1895) 97; Capt. J.J. Womack, *The Civil War Diary of Capt. J.J. Womack*, typescript, n.d., n.p. PBSHS.

14. *OR*, 16(1):1120-22; Unidentified diary, Thirty-third Alabama Infantry File, PBSHS.

15. *Ibid.* 16(1):1124-34; N.E. Yeatman, Address to Confederate Veterans, qtd. in *Knoxville Sentinel*, n.d. in Scrapbook, U.D.C., Helena Ark, cited in Howell and Elizabeth Purdue, *Pat Cleburne: Confederate General* (Tuscaloosa: Portals Press, 1977) 89.

16. *Ibid.* 16(1):1122-24.

17. *Ibid.* 16(1):1122-24, 1127.

18. *Ibid.* 16(1):1047, 1050.

19. General J.A. Chalaron, "Last Guns in Battle at Perryville, Ky.," *New Orleans Times-Picayune*, November 25, 1906.

20. *Ibid.*

21. *Ibid.*

22. *OR,* 16(1):1123-24.

23. *Ibid.,* 1093-94.

24. *Ibid.,* 1123; Statement written by Col. J.A. Chalaron, *New Orleans Times-Picayune*, n.d., LHAP, H-TML, TU. Chalaron's statement recounts the whole story of Lieutenant Blair's transport of Mary Henry Lyon Jones's flag home to Mobile, Alabama.

25. Statement written by Col. J.A. Chalaron, *New Orleans Times-Picayune*, n.d., LHAP, H-TML, TU.

Epilogue

1. Hughes, *The Pride of the Confederate Artillery*, 79-92, 123-46.

2. J.A. Chalaron, "Louisiana at Chickamauga," *New Orleans Times-Picayune*, September 21, 1913; Lieutenant Thomas Blair plot, Spring Hill Cemetery, Mobile, Alabama. Blair's headstone incorrectly states September 20, 1863, as the date of his death; it was actually September 19.

3. Chalaron, "Louisiana at Chickamauga;" Hughes, *The Pride of the Confederate Artillery*, 164-72.

4. Hughes, *The Pride of the Confederate Artillery*, 228-35.

5. *Ibid.*, 266-73.

6. Printer, *The City Intelligencer, or Stranger's Guide*, 4.

7. Amelia Gorgas, "The Evacuation of Richmond: Personal Recollections of Mrs. Amelia Gorgas as Recorded in Her Diary," *Confederate Veteran*, 25 (1917) 110-11.

8. *Ibid.*

9. *Ibid.*

10 "Genealogy of John Tyler and His Descendants," Sherwood Forest Plantation Foundation, http://www.sherwoodforest.org/Genealogy.html; Verbon E. Kemp, ed., *The Alumni Directory and Service Record of Washington and Lee University*. (Lexington: The Alumni Incorporated, 1926) 1261. The diploma of David Gardiner Tyler from Washington College awarding him a bachelor of law degree, signed by Robert E. Lee as president of the college, is in the possession of Mary M. Booth, Lynchburg, Virginia. Ms. Booth is Mary Henry Lyon Jones's great-granddaughter and granddaughter of David Gardiner Tyler and Mary Morris Jones Tyler; Elizabeth Wright Weddell, *St. Paul's Church, Richmond, Virginia: Its Historic Years and Memorials*, 2 vols. (Richmond: The William Byrd Press, 1931) II, 508, 600.

11. Hollywood Cemetery, James Alfred Jones and Mary Henry Lyon Jones plots; *In Memoriam: Mary Henry Jones*, VSL; The Richmond *Whig*, April 4, 1886; The Richmond *Dispatch*, March 30, 1866.

Bibliography

Newspapers
Baltimore Sun
Charleston Daily Courier
Charleston Mercury
Illustrated London News
New Orleans Daily Picauyne
New Orleans Times-Picayune
New York Herald
New York Times
Frank Leslie's Illustrated Newspaper
Richmond Dispatch
Richmond Enquirer
Richmond Whig
Wadesboro *North Carolina Argus*

Government Publications
Journal of the Congress of the Confederate States of America (1861), 5 vols. (Washington: Government Printing Office, 1904).
The War of the Rebellion: A Compilation of the Official Records of the Union and Confederate Armies, 128 vols. (Washington, DC, 1880-1901).

Books
Bonner, Robert E. *Colors and Blood: Flag Passions of the Confederate South.* Princeton: Princeton University Press, 2004.

Blackford, Susan Leigh, comp. *Memoirs of Life In and Out of the Army in Virginia During the War Between the States*, 2 vols. Lynchburg: J.P. Bell, 1894.

Cannon, Devereaux D., Jr. *The Flags of the Confederacy: An Illustrated History.* Memphis: St. Luke's Press, 1988.

Claiborne, John Herbert. *Petersburg in the 1850's.* Marvin T. Boyhill, III, ed. Petersburg: Appomattox Iron Works, 1993.

Coski, John W. *The Confederate Battle Flag: America's Most Embattled Emblem.* Cambridge, MA: Belknap Press of Harvard University Press, 2005.

Current, Richard N. ed. *Encyclopedia of the Confederacy*, 4 vols. New York: Simon and Schuster, 1993.

Davis, William C. *Battle at Bull Run: A History of the First Major Campaign of the Civil War.* New York: Doubleday, 1977.

Dickert, Augustus D. *History of Kershaw's Brigade.* Dayton: Press of Morningside Bookshop, 1976.

Douglas, Henry Kyd. *I Rode With Stonewall.* Chapel Hill: University of North Carolina Press, 1940.

du Bellet, Louise Pequet et al. *Some Prominent Virginia Families*, 4 vols. Lynchburg: J.P. Bell, 1907.

Hanson, Joseph Mills. *Bull Run Remembers: History, Traditions and Landmarks of the Manassas (Bull Run) Campaign Before Washington 1861-1862.* Manassas, VA: National Capital, 1957.

Head, Thomas D. *Campaigns and Battles of the Sixteenth Tennessee Infantry.* Nashville: Cumberland Presbyterian Pub., 1895.

Harrison, Mrs. Burton. *Recollections Grave and Gay.* New York: Charles Scribner's Sons, 1911.

Howard, McHenry. *Recollections of a Maryland Confederate Soldier and Staff Officer Under Johnston, Jackson and Lee.* Dayton: Press of Morningside Bookshop, 1975.

Hughes, Nathanial Cheairs, Jr. *The Pride of the Confederate Artillery: The Washington Artillery in the Army of the Tennessee.* Baton Rouge: Louisiana State University Press, 1997.

John Milner Associates. *Fairfax County Civil War Sites Inventory.* Fairfax County, VA: Fairfax County Board of Supervisors, August 2002.

Johnston, Joseph E. *Narrative of Military Operations, Directed, During the Late War Between the States.* New York: D. Appleton and Company, 1874.

Kemp, Verbon E., ed. *The Alumni Directory and Service Record of Washington and Lee University.* Lexington: The Alumni Incorporated, 1926.

Krick, Robert E.L. *Staff Officers in Gray: A Biographical Register of the Staff Officers in the Army of Northern Virginia.* Chapel Hill: University of North Carolina Press, 2009.

Krick, Robert K. *Lee's Colonels: A Biographical Register of the Field Officers of the Army of Northern Virginia.* Dayton: Press of Morningside Bookshop, 1979.

Lee, Charles Robert, Jr. *The Confederate Constitutions.* Chapel Hill: University of North Carolina Press, 1863.

Leonard, Cynthia Miller, comp. *The General Assembly of Virginia, July 30, 1619—January 11, 1978.* Richmond: Virginia State Library, 1978.

Lesser, Charles H. *Relic of the Lost Cause: The Story of South Carolina's Ordinance of Secession.* Columbia: South Carolina Department of Archives and History, 1996.

Madaus, Howard Michael and Robert D. Needham. *The Battle Flags of the Confederate Army of Tennessee.* Milwaukee: Milwaukee Public Museum, 1976.

Miller, Francis Trevelyan. *The Photographic History of the Civil War*, 10 vols. New York: Review of Reviews, 1911.

Morgan, W.H. *Personal Reminiscences of the War of 1861-5.* Lynchburg: J.P. Bell, 1911.

Potter, David M. *The Impending Crisis, 1848-1861.* New York: Harper and Row, 1976.

Printer, *The City Intelligencer; Or, Stranger's Guide.* Richmond: McFarlane and Ferguson, Printers, 1862.

Purdue, Howell and Elizabeth. *Pat Cleburne: Confederate General.* Tuscaloosa: Portals Press, 1977.

Reid, J.W. *History of the Fourth Regiment of South Carolina Volunteers.* Dayton: Press of Morningside Bookshop, 1975.

Rogers, William Warren, Jr. *Confederate Homefront: Montgomery During the Civil War.* Tuscaloosa: University of Alabama Press, 1999.

Roman, Alfred. *The Military Operations of General Beauregard In The War Between the States, 1861-1865*, 2 vols. New York: Harper and Brothers, 1884.

Severens, Kenneth. *Charleston Antebellum Architecture and Civic Destiny.* Knoxville: University of Tennessee Press, 1988.

Sorrel, Brig. Gen. G. Moxley . *Recollections of a Confederate Staff Officer.* Bell Irvin Wiley, ed. Jackson: McCowat-Mercer, 1958.

Thomas, Emory M. *The Confederate Nation, 1861-1865.* New York: Harper and Row, 1979.

Tyler, Lyon Gardiner, LLD. *Encyclopedia of Virginia Biography.* New York: Lewis Historical Pub., 1915.

Waddell, Elizabeth Wright. *St. Paul's Church, Richmond, Virginia: Its Historic Years and Memorials*, 2 vols. Richmond: William Byrd, 1931.

War Department, *Regulations of the Army of the Confederate States, 1863.* Richmond: J.W. Randolph, 1863.

Warner, Ezra J. *Generals in Blue: Lives of the Union Commanders.* Baton Rouge: Louisiana State University Press, 1964.

———. *Generals in Gray: Lives of the Confederate Commanders.* Baton Rouge: Louisiana State University Press, 1959.

Watkins, Sam. *Company Aytch: A Side Show of the Big Show.* Bell Irvin Wiley, ed. Jackson: McCowat-Mercer, 1952.

Womack, Capt. J.J. *The Civil War Diary of Capt. J.J. Womak,* typescript, n.d., n.p. PBSHS.

Van Woodwoard, C. *Mary Chesnut's Civil War.* New Haven: Yale University Press, 1981.

Articles

Beauregard, G.T. "The First Battle of Bull Run," Robert Underwood Johnson and Clarence Clough Buel, eds. *Battles and Leaders of the Civil War*, 4 vols. New York: Thomas Yoseloff. I: 196-228.

Brock, John Brighton. "Symbols of a Nation: The First Flag of the Confederacy Made in Montgomery." *Alabama Living* (March 2011), 16-18.

Cabell, W.L. "True History of Our Battle Flag." *Confederate Veteran:* 11 (1903), 339-40.

Cary, Roger D. "Belle Run." *Baltimore Sun* (October 25, 2000).

Chalaron, General J.A. "Last Guns in Battle at Perryville, Ky." *New Orleans Times-Picayune*, November 25, 1906.

Coleman, Elizabeth Dabney. "The Captain Was a Lady." *Virginia Cavalcade:* 6 (Summer 1956-Spring 1957), 35-41.

Dawson, Francis W. "Letters of a British Officer in the Confederacy."

Editor. "The Confederate Flag." *Southern Historical Society Papers:* 8 (1880), 155-57.

Editor. "The Fifth Company, Washington Artillery." *New Orleans Times-Picayune*, March 10, 1902.

Gorgas, Amelia. "The Evacuation of Richmond: Personal Recollections of Mrs. Amelia Gorgas as Recorded in Her Diary." *Confederate Veteran:* 25 (1917), 110-11.

Griggs, Walter S., Jr. "The Cary Invincibles." Richmond Guide (Spring 2011). http://trendmag2.trendoffset.com/display_article.php?id=686106.

Harrison, Constance Cary. "Virginia Scenes in '61," Robert Underwood Johnson and Clarence Clough Buel, eds. *Battles and Leaders of the Civil War*, 4 vols. New York: Thomas Yoseloff, 1956: I:160-66.

McCarthy, Charleton. "Origin of the Confederate Battle Flag." *Southern Historical Society Papers:* 8 (1880), 197-99.

Reiner, Karl. "The House of Shattered Dreams." September 29, 2004. http://www.connectionnewspapers.com/news/2004/sep/29/the-house-of-shattered-dreams/.

Stevenson, P.D. "The Fifth Company, Washington Artillery." *New Orleans Times-Picayune*, March 10, 1902.

University of Virginia, "Carr's Hill." Last modified August 27, 2009. http://www.virginia.edu/carrshill/jefferson.html.

Archival Materials
Alabama
William M. Lyon, Jr., Mobile
The Letters of Mary Henry Lyon Jones
"My Dear Parent" from Mary, July 28, 1859

Kentucky
Perryville Battlefield State Historic Site
Unidentified diary, Thirty-third Alabama Infantry File

Louisiana
Tulane University, New Orleans
Louisiana Historical Association Papers
J.B. Walton to G.T. Beauregard, January 30, 1872
Jubal A. Early to Jefferson Davis, December 30, 1878
Collin McRae Selph to Col. J.A. Chalaron, July 25, 1905
G.T. Beauregard to G.H. Preble, January 24, 1872

G.W. Smith to G.T. Beauregard, January 15, 1872
W.L. Cabell to Col. J.A. Chalaron, August 5, 1903

Nebraska
Lon W. Keim, M.D., Omaha
Fonda G. Thomsen to Lon W. Keim, MD, "Analysis Report," April 20, 1996.

Virginia
Mary Morris Booth, Lynchburg
Letters of James Alfred Jones
"Dear Mary" from "Devoted Husband," May 24, 1862
"My Dear Mary" from "Your ever devoted husband," May 25, 1862
Lewis Leigh, Jr., Leesburg
Original *General Order No. 75, November 28, 1861*
Original Jennie Cary to General Beauregard, dated December 12, 1861
Original (field copy) General Beauregard to Jennie Cary, dated December 15, 1861
Manassas National Battlefield, Manassas
Map Showing the Confederate Encampments Around Centreville, 1861-1862
Museum of the Confederacy, Richmond
G.T. Beauregard to William Porcher Miles, August 27, 1861
"To Molly" Letters: Sam Payne to Cousin (Mollie), December 1, 1861
Virginia State Library, Richmond
In Memoriam, Mary Henry Jones (died March 20, 1886), n.p., n.d.
James Alfred Jones L.L.D. typescript, n.p., n.d.

Miscellaneous Sources
American Civil War Forum. Last modified 2012. http://www. americancivilwarforum.com/letters-of-francis-w.-dawson-british-officer-in-the-confederacy-1353418.html.
"Confederate Battle Flags' History–1 (U.S.)," Museum of the Confederacy, last modified October 15, 2010, http://www. crwflags.com/fotw/flags/us-csah.html.

"Constance Cary Harrison," *Wikipedia,* last modified August 13 2013, http://en.wikipedia.org/wiki/Constance_Cary_Harrison.

"CSA Dealer, Items for Sale," Patricia A. Kaufmann, accessed August 1, 2013, http://www.csadealer.com/items-for-sale.

"Hetty Cary, JHBL Family Genealogy," http://www.latrobefamily.com/genealogy/getperson.php?personID=I5349&tree=mytree.

"Francis Strother Lyon," *Wikipedia,* last modified March 16, 2013, http://en.wikipedia.org/wiki/Francis_Strother_Lyon.

"Nicola Marschall," *Wikipedia,* last modified March 17, 2013, http://en.wikipedia.org/wiki/Nicola_Marschall.

Richmond City Business Directory, 1860, n.p., http://www.mdgorman.com.

"Robert T. Jones, Cullum's Register, 903," last modified March 5, 2013, http://penelope.uchicago.edu/Thayer/E/Gazetteer/Places/America/United_States/Army/USMA/Cullums_Register/903*.html.

"Saltire," *Wikipedia*, last modified September 15, 2013, https://en.wikipedia.org/wiki/Saltire.

Index